Sex and Death

For Bob

Sex and Death

A Reappraisal of Human Mortality

Beverley Clack

polity

First published in 2002 by Polity Press in association with Blackwell Publishers Ltd

Editorial office:
Polity Press
65 Bridge Street
Cambridge CB2 1UR, UK

Marketing and production:
Blackwell Publishers Ltd
108 Cowley Road
Oxford OX4 1JF, UK

Published in the USA by
Blackwell Publishers Inc.
350 Main Street
Malden, MA 02148, USA

A catalogue record for this book is available from the British Library.

Library of Congress Cataloging-in-Publication Data

Clack, Beverley.
    Sex and death : a reappraisal of human mortality / Beverley Clack.
        p.   cm.
    Includes bibliographical references (p.   ) and index.
    ISBN 0–7456–2278–X — ISBN 0–7456–2279–8 (pbk.)
    1. Death.   2. Mortality.   I. Title.
    BD444.C58 2002
    128'.—dc21   2001007561

Typeset in 10.5 on 12.5 pt Sabon
by Ace Filmsetting Ltd, Frome, Somerset
Printed in Great Britain by MPG Books Ltd, Bodmin, Cornwall

This book is printed on acid-free paper.

Contents

Acknowledgements

This book has been some time in the making, and, in common with other projects conceived and executed over a number of years, has benefited from discussions with and suggestions from others. At the outset I would like to thank Rebecca Harkin for commissioning it, and for her continuing interest in the project. Thanks are due particularly to my brother, Brian R. Clack, for borrowings from his extensive library, for his sharp mind, and for the illuminating discussions we have had on this and related topics. I am indebted to him especially for his suggestions regarding Sade. Gwen Griffith-Dickson was a diligent reader of the typescript, and her suggestions have considerably strengthened significant parts of my thesis. Caroline Richmond was a painstakingly accurate copy-editor whose attention to detail has clarified some of my more impenetrable sentences. I would like to thank Pamela Sue Anderson for her interest in and support of this work, and for her continuing friendship. Thanks, too, to Yvonne Sherwood for discussions on excrement; to Lisa Isherwood for her support and encouragement; to Philippa Donald for discussions of Freud and psychoanalysis, and for being a good friend; to Harriet Harris and Angie Pears for helpful conversations and for the opportunity to try out ideas; and to Grace Jantzen for her significant work in the feminist philosophy of religion. My colleagues at the University of Surrey, Roehampton, have also been an invaluable source of support, and have listened to this work at various stages in its development. Thanks are due in particular to David Hill for his insights as to definitions of transcendence, and to Anne Spalding for her discussions of Christianity.

I am fortunate that all of those mentioned above can be called friends.

In addition, I would like to thank my family, especially my parents, Ann Clack and Alan Clack, and my sister-in-law, Deborah Shaer, for their love and support. Thanks, too, to Sarah Claridge, Jane Corrin, Mark O'Rourke, Mariam Rosser-Owen and Kent Rawlinson for their friendship. And finally, I would like to dedicate this book to my husband, Robert Lindsey, who edited the passages from Shakespeare and checked obscure references, and whose love, support, and commitment made its writing possible.

Introduction

Shakespeare's King Lear, confronted by Edgar in his guise as mad Tom, reflects on this half-naked figure as an example of humanity stripped down to the essentials:

> Is man no more than this? Consider him well. Thou ow'st the worm no silk, the beast no hide, the sheep no wool, the cat no perfume. Ha! Here's three on's are sophisticated; thou art the thing itself. Unaccommodated man is no more but such a poor, bare, forked animal as thou art. (*King Lear* 3.4)

What is it to be a human being? When we strip away the centuries of Western intellectual enquiry, we are left with three undeniable facts: that we are animals who are born, who reproduce sexually, and who will die. The aim of this book is to focus on what might be considered the key elements of this cycle: sex and death.[1] If we take seriously the role that these features play in defining our existence – indeed, if we allow these factors to speak to us about the nature of our existence – must this rule out the possibility of any deep understanding of our place in the world? In other words, must an emphasis on such features exclude the possibility of a meaningful approach to human life? Or, to put it another way, is it possible to base a spiritually fulfilling life upon these basic physical facts?

Let me clarify what I mean when I use that word 'spiritual'. As we shall see, there has been a tendency to understand spirituality as a feature of life that is radically distinct from ordinary physical existence. Commonly, the word demarcates a lifestyle based upon a transcendent other, a lifestyle which is grounded in specific religious practices. I shall use it rather differently, relating it to the attempt to create meaning through a reflective engagement with the world. As such, I am adopting Pierre Hadot's account of 'the spiritual' as the most appropriate term for describing this quest for meaning. Hadot suggests something of the paucity of the other expressions available to us for describing this deep engagement with the different aspects of being human: 'None of the other adjectives we would use – "psychic", "moral", "ethical", "intellectual", "of thought", "of the soul", – covers all the aspects of reality we want to describe"' (Hadot 1995: 81).

I would tend to agree with his analysis, although the emphasis I shall place upon that word 'spiritual' is rather different, and involves exploring the varied attempts made by human beings to live in such a way that the physical experience of being human is endowed with meaning. As such, I shall tend to use the terms 'spirituality' and 'the meaningful life' interchangeably, for, as I hope will become apparent, my claim is that the only meaningful life is the one which engages with the depths open to human beings. In using this word 'depth', I am thinking of the profundity accessible to us when we engage reflectively with the world around us. The kind of contemplation I am envisaging is one that will neither exclude the sexual nor evade the issue of mortality, but through focusing on these features will be able to derive from them a deeper understanding of the possibilities open to humanity. Contemplation has clearly played a significant role in establishing what might be called 'Western spirituality', and as such it will be impossible to avoid engaging with aspects of the Christian tradition and thus with issues which have usually been discussed under the remit of 'religion'. I shall suggest, however, that it is not only by embracing a religious tradition that one can achieve a meaningful life in the face of our human physicality and all that this implies. An engagement with what it means to be human can open the way to a fuller understanding of the place of our existence in the broader context of the universe that need not be located in any given religious tradition.

All of this suggests that the account of the spiritual or meaningful life I shall be advocating will avoid placing such a lifestyle outside the ordinary experience of being human. If for Augustine, the great Christian theologian whose work was to inform the shape of both Catholic and Protestant theology, the spiritual life involves resisting the sexual in order to conquer death, I shall argue that it is only by accepting that we are sexual and mortal beings that we shall be able to construct a truly meaningful life.

Before we can move to consider what such a life might involve, it is worth being aware of a powerful trend in Western thinking that links sex and death together. It is a connection that arises in different contexts and in the ideas of different, sometimes radically diverse, philosophies. As we shall see, Augustine is not alone in making this association when he outlines his approach to both God and the spiritual life. Rather than see sexuality as something altogether different from death, linked with the processes of new life, an explicit connection has been made between human sexuality and the inevitability of death. This is expressed poetically, and powerfully, in some of the key myths that have informed the cultural background for the tradition. Describing the birth of the gods in his *Theogony*, the Greek poet Hesiod quickly turns his attention to Eros, the god of sexual love.[2] The physical attributes of such a god are much as one would expect: Eros is 'the most handsome among the immortal gods'; but Hesiod goes on to suggest that this same Eros possesses attributes associated with death and chaos. Eros is the 'dissolver of flesh, who overcomes reason and purpose in the breasts of all gods and all men' (Hesiod 1988: 6). While sex might bring life – and indeed Hesiod introduces Eros early on in his account in order to explain the births of the other gods – it is also potentially destructive. Reflection on the experience of sexual love suggests that in such acts there is a pre-empting of the dissolution of the flesh after death. Just as personal boundaries are dissolved into the other during intercourse, so death will instigate the dissolution of the flesh. Similarly, the experience of *eros* brings with it disruption to the life of the mind: it is all too easy for Eros to destroy the order of life.[3]

In Hesiod's *Works and Days*, a different emphasis is placed upon this story. If love and death have already been given a strange kinship, Hesiod builds upon this alliance and gives it a gendered interpretation. As we shall see, the connection between women, sex and death underpins some of the disparate theories of Western thinking.[4] Hesiod presents the story of Pandora, the first woman, as the explanation for the evils that afflict humanity. Zeus has Hephaestus make earth and water into a human figure modelled on the immortal goddesses. She is given all the gifts the immortals can bestow: charm, beauty, grace, desire. But at the same time she is given 'a bitch's mind and a knavish nature' (Hesiod 1988: 39), which seems to concur with later ideas of female beauty hiding the worst aspects of humanity.[5] Sent to earth to be 'a calamity for men who live by bread' (Hesiod 1988: 39), Pandora is given a honey vase (or _pithos_) filled not with blesses, but with curses. Unable to contain her curiosity, she opens the vase and lets out its contents: pain, sickness and death. Only Hope remains, trapped in the jar.

That Pandora is given such a vessel suggests a fundamental connection between woman, sex and death – a connection that arises frequently and in different forms in the later thinkers of the Western tradition.[6] Hesiod describes Pandora in deliberately sexual language. She is as beautiful as a goddess, as deceitful as a bitch. That she carries a vessel itself resonates with ideas of woman as womb, as a container for new life. Yet that vessel/womb also contains mortality: hence, while woman is the giver of life, she is also the bringer of death.

This connection between woman, sex and death is also identifiable in the Judeo-Christian tradition with the biblical story of Adam and Eve (Genesis 2: 5–3: 24). It is difficult to overestimate the significance that this story has had for the Western conception of humanity.[7] Having created human beings and placed them in the Garden of Eden, God commands them not to eat from the tree of the knowledge of good and evil: to do so will mean death. The woman is approached by the serpent who challenges this dictum; encouraged by his words, she sees that the fruit of the tree is good to eat, and does so, giving some to her husband. Upon eating the fruit they become aware of their nakedness; ashamed, they make loincloths with which to cover themselves. God, on discovering what they have done, curses them – the woman to pain in childbirth, the man to the necessity of labour – and dismisses them from the garden.

The structure of the story thus makes an implicit connection between woman and death. Eve is the one approached by the serpent; it is she who takes the forbidden fruit and eats, thus letting death into the world. Moreover, the curse placed upon Eve suggests that woman is peculiarly connected to sex: not only is her punishment linked to her procreative function, she is also told that, despite the pain of childbirth, 'your desire shall be for your husband' (Genesis 3: 16).

Given this context, it should not surprise us that various forms of the spiritual or meaningful life will suggest that sex is problematic, for it has intimations of the horrors of death. My intention is to resist this conclusion, and, while I think it is important to make connections between sexuality and mortality (both features telling us much about the nature of our humanity), I shall argue that a meaningful account of human existence must be predicated upon a recognition *and acceptance* of the sexuate and mortal nature of human being.

In order to establish such a conclusion, I shall engage with the works of seven philosophers whose concepts sometimes support, sometimes challenge, but ultimately clarify what such a form of life might involve. In using the ideas of Plato, Augustine, Jean-Paul Sartre, Simone de Beauvoir, Sigmund Freud, the Marquis de Sade and Seneca, I have not sought to provide a historical account of the Western attitude towards and understanding of sex and death. Rather, my interest is in using aspects of their thought to develop my own argument.[8] As such, the structure of this book is determined not by chronology, but by the way in which the ideas of these seven figures advance my own argument; namely that a meaningful life can be based upon a recognition of our basic humanity. We are sexuate and mortal animals; but accepting this conclusion need not lead to a sense that there is no meaning beyond the basic facts of physicality. Indeed, I shall argue that it is through reflection on sex and death that we can derive a meaningful account of what it is to be human.

In seeking to claim that it is possible to accept the fact that we are both sexual and mortal beings, *and* to formulate a meaningful life based upon these facts, it is necessary to consider the interplay of the ideas of transcendence and immanence as they have been applied in accounts of human being. In applying such terms to the construct of human being, I am using Simone de Beauvoir's analysis: that human being is defined both by an ability to go beyond its physical placing (transcendence) and by its physical placing (immanence). It is the interplay between these two features that governs the structure of this work. In various ways, the different figures employed by this study illuminate and challenge accounts of human being that focus on one aspect at the expense of the other; their advocacy of one or the other leads to different, and sometimes polarized, ideas about the issues raised by sexuality and mortality.

There has, then, been a tendency to describe human being in terms that emphasize either the transcendent or the immanent aspect. This has led to a polarization between these two features. In areas as diverse as Augustine's theology and Sartre's existentialism the attempt has been made to distance us from what might be called the animal aspects of our existence. Thus emphasis has been placed upon the attempt to *transcend* the basic physical facts of human existence: namely that we reproduce by sexual intercourse, and that we are mutable, fleshly beings who will ultimately die. In the philosophy of Plato, this attempt at transcendence takes the form of prioritizing the life of the mind over physical existence. In the formulation of Augustine's theology this view is developed, and an explicit connection is made between sexuality and mortality: transcend the sexual and you can transcend the rule of death. The ideas of Plato and Augustine have been highly influential, determining the shape of Western thinking regarding sex and death and the structure that has been imposed upon the spiritual life. It is for this reason that this study will begin with an exploration of their views. Having established the approach that they take, we will turn our attention to Sartre and Beauvoir.

This might seem a strange move to make: after all, there seems to be little similarity or connection between the ideas of these twentieth-century existentialist philosophers and the classical ideas of Plato and Augustine. Yet when we analyse the philosophies of Sartre and Beauvoir, there are surprising similarities. For the existentialist, *the* human project is identified with the attempt to 'stand out' from the world. This attempt is linked with the desire to transcend those features that show us to be, in fact, animals, albeit animals with a peculiar bent – what Freud might call the fact that, as animals who have developed self-reflectivity, we are 'neurotic animals'. In Freud's schema, we cannot accept our animal nature, illustrated most graphically in the experiences of sex and death, and thus we are doomed to unhappiness, stuck as we are between heaven and earth. Sartre's philosophy attempts to distance the concept of humanity from its animal grounding, and surprisingly, despite his advocacy of humanism, there are considerable similarities to be discerned between his ideas and those of Plato and Augustine. According to Sartre (and also Beauvoir), human being is defined not by its physical placing in the world, but by its ability to transcend that placing. In considering the prevalence of ideas which postulate transcendence as an escape from our mortality, my aim is to challenge the argument that a meaningful account of human life can be achieved only if our sexual embodiment and the fact that we will die are eclipsed by some other 'greater' goal or purpose. For Plato, this goal is defined as attaining the world of ideas or forms; for Augustine, it is the attainment of the transcendent God. For Sartre and Beauvoir, it is found in the freedom to shape one's life and thoughts.

Transcendence, and even a form of immortality, for Sartre at least, is found through the written word.

All of which necessitates some reflection on alternative ways of thinking that emphasize the *immanent*: that is, the physical, immediately discernible aspects of being a human animal. Of crucial importance to any contemporary attempt to deal with the themes of sex and death is the work of Sigmund Freud. Freud's account of the human self emphasizes and prioritizes the unconscious and the instinctual. If we are really to understand what it is to be a human being, we must be aware of the power of the sex- and death-drives that determine our human responses to life. It is precisely these features that hold the key to our humanity. In drawing our attention to the crucial role played by both sexuality and death for defining who we are, Freud's account runs contrary to those of the theorists whose ideas of selfhood emphasize the centrality of rationality, autonomy and individuality. For Freud, an account of the human self that stresses such features deals only with the surface level of our humanity. Under his reading, the structuring of both human society and human individuality involves a constant struggle to master the unruly elements lurking beneath the manufactured ego. Freud seems to be saying that we are animals, and the only way to live a happy or meaningful life is to accept that this is the case.

Such claims challenge the idea that we could construct some kind of spirituality that offers a way of living a fulfilling life in the face of human mortality. The ideals that have formed the basis of previous accounts of the spiritual cohere easily with the qualities of the autonomous, rational, free self that Freud's account implicitly challenges. For this reason, Freud's ideas are placed at the centre of this book, for he challenges the very basis for an account that argues that the meaningful life could be based upon some transcendent feature of our humanity. In addressing his ideas, I want to ask what would happen if we took Freud's claims seriously. Would it still be possible to craft a vision of our humanity that stressed the depths and profundity of life, while maintaining the reality of our connection with the rest of the animal world? As we shall see, Freud himself seems to suggest that this might be possible, and in some places he even seems to suggest an account of the meaningful life which breaks down the polarization between transcendent and immanent accounts of human being. He suggests that an acceptance of ordinary, mutable human existence could be used as the basis for an aesthetic response to the world. Indeed, an appreciation of beauty – dare one say life itself – might be possible only through an acceptance of the vulnerability and transience of human existence. A form of transcendence could then be developed which was located in the physical processes and cycles of the natural world.

Reflection on Freud will necessitate renewed consideration of the relationship between transcendence and immanence. If we accept the facts of human mortality, are we inevitably led to a valueless and meaningless universe? Freud suggests that this need not be the case, but it is important to test his thesis by pushing it as far as it will go. If we locate meaning in an acceptance of the physical processes of existence, what kind of lifestyle do we arrive at? It is significant that one of the foremost figures who links sex and death – the Marquis de Sade – goes on to present a hellish vision of a world which eschews transcendence, a world in which there is no moral difference between the slicing of an aubergine and the mutilation of a child. Sade's universe is based upon an acceptance of physical life and the rejection of any kind of transcendent value. Human life is located simply within the physical processes of the universe. It would seem that the moral consequences of rejecting any transcendent dimension are far-reaching and terrifying.

Stepping through the looking glass into Sade's predatory and horrifying world may make us long for the old sureties of transcendent value offered by Plato and Augustine. Yet seeking to establish some kind of value system need not necessitate a return to the old idea of transcendence as something imposed upon the world from without. There are other ways of defining transcendence, ways that do not neglect the significance of those immanent features that determine our humanity. A less dualistic, more unified account of immanence and transcendence that escapes polarizing the physical and reflective aspects of our humanity might be possible.

In seeking to combat Sade's decidedly pessimistic view, the ideas of the Roman philosopher Seneca prove useful for developing a balanced account of human life that includes transcendent and immanent features. Seneca's philosophy is predicated upon the claim that to live 'the good life' entails 'living in accordance with nature'. 'Nature' in this context includes rationality, and I shall argue that the application of this idea breaks down dualistic accounts of the transcendent which view this as standing in opposition to physical human life. The transcendent becomes less something defined in opposition to the features of ordinary human life, and more a facet or way of being to be discovered through the very ordinariness of being human. Seneca's ideas pave the way for a meaningful life that is based upon the facts of our humanity: that we are sexuate and mortal beings. But that is not all we are. We are also beings who are open to both relationship and reflection: and it is through reflection on the aspects of ordinary human life – the reality and necessity of sexual intercourse and the inevitability of death – that we can arrive at this conclusion. Rather than postulating transcendence at the expense of immanence, Seneca's Stoicism shows a way of holding both aspects together, thus indicating the possibility of a fulfilled, complete and integrated human life.

Having employed the ideas of these seven philosophers to develop and challenge the possibility of a this-worldly spirituality, I shall end with some suggestions for how to live a meaningful life. My intention is to explore the way in which reflection on sexuality and mortality can provide the basis for an understanding of human life placed squarely in this world. Reflection on sexuality challenges overly individualistic accounts of what it means to be human, highlighting the significance of relationship for understanding our humanity. Reflection on mortality will challenge us to think more deeply about life and what, ultimately, might be considered meaningful in the face of our inevitable demise. We must engage with both the vulnerability and the tragedy of our humanity. And, I shall argue, it is only by so doing that we might get closer to the depth open to us as human beings who are reflective and relational.

An adequate contemporary spirituality must, then, be grounded in a well-rounded and inclusive account of our humanity, and thus must include engaging with death as well as life. Reflection on the most basic aspects of our humanity can achieve a sense of life's profundity, but a profundity that does not seek to gloss over the difficult and tragic elements of being human. In accepting the facts of human existence, meaning and value is still possible, and it is with this hope in mind that this study has been attempted.

1

Transcending Mortality: Plato's Philosophy and Augustine's Theology

Introduction

> For, indeed, when, where and how can what are called the primary objects of nature be possessed in this life with such certainty that they are not subject to the vicissitudes of chance? For is there any pain, the contrary of pleasure, any disquiet, the contrary of rest, that cannot befall a wise man's body? (*City of God*, XIX, 4; Augustine 1998: 919).

These words from Augustine could well describe the challenge that faces both himself and Plato when formulating their respective philosophies of life. When confronted with the mutability and transience of human life, they seek to employ methods which ground the meaningful existence in a transcendent other: for Plato, the solution to this problem lies in postulating an eternal realm which transcends this world of mutable appearance, and which, through philosophical training, one might attain in the here and now. For Augustine, the solution to the transitory nature of this world is found in the eternal God.

It is hard to overestimate the influence that these figures have had upon the development of Western philosophy and theology. It has become something of a cliché to note A. N. Whitehead's description of Western philosophy as nothing more than a series of footnotes to

Plato's philosophy (cf. Flew 1989: 41), while Augustine's theology has shaped both Catholic and Protestant doctrine. They are similarly important for this study, in that their approach to sex and death has affected the way in which accounts of the human individual and the divine have developed in Western thought. It is for this reason that they form the starting point for this engagement with sex and death. To a greater and lesser extent, they have suggested that the facts of sex and death need to be transcended if one is to live a meaningful life. Their influence is to be found in the subsequent way in which spirituality has been defined and understood in the Western tradition. Invariably the spiritual life and what it entails has been distanced from what might be considered the basic experience of being human: that we replicate through sexual intercourse, and that we will all die. My intention in this chapter is to engage with their ideas, and, while I shall be at pains to identify this attempt to define the spiritual life according to the ability to transcend one's human placing, I shall also suggest that, within both schemes of thought, counter-trends can be identified which support the possibility of alternative ways of structuring meaning and the spiritual life. It may be possible to develop an account of meaning which does not attempt to deny 'the vicissitudes of chance', but instead grounds the meaning of human life in the cycles and movements attested to by the phenomena of sexuality and mortality.

Sex and death in Plato

Plato's philosophical dualism has in recent years been both challenged and criticized, particularly by feminist writers (see Annas 1981; Plumwood 1993; Cavarero 1995). For some, the main concern has been with the implications that this radical division of human experience has had for women's lives, and for the way in which the planet is approached.[1] While the insights of feminist commentators have influenced my response to his philosophy, my principal interest is to draw out the implications of Platonic dualism for understandings of sexuality and mortality. The idea that what is meaningful about human life is that which transcends these features can be traced to his ideas. However, I shall also highlight those elements in his thought that suggest a more positive account of the role that might be played by the physical.

Plato's understanding of the nature of reality effectively turns our commonsense perception of things on its head; or, as Luce Irigaray puts it, the world is 'turned upside-down and back-to-front' (Irigaray 1985a: 244). Plato contends that the physical world is but a pale reflection of reality; that we live in a world of appearance, contrasted with the absolute truth of the world of Forms or Ideas, which transcends this world. In *The Republic*, Plato gives the clearest and most detailed account of this dualistic worldview. His analogy of the Cave (*Republic,* VII, 514a–521b) suggests a definite distinction between this physical world of shadowy impressions and the 'real' world of ideas. Plato describes the human condition as similar to that of prisoners kept in an underground cave. A fire has been lit behind them, and they have been bound so that they can see only the wall that lies immediately before them. Shadows are cast upon the wall by puppets manipulated by the guards. The prisoners think that this is all there is: as Julia Annas points out, Plato is at pains to detail the bewilderment the majority would experience if forced to confront the pitiful way in which they live their lives (Annas 1981: 252). Only a few are prepared to accept that they are living an impoverished existence and wish to cast off their bonds and escape from the cave into the sunlight of the real world. This analogy informs Plato's account of philosophy: only the philosopher is capable of rejecting appearance in favour of a genuine engagement with the true nature of reality. In this sense, accepting the existence of the Forms that lie beyond the appearance of life in this world is rather like a religious conversion (Annas 1981: 238).

> Similarly, if someone fails to realize that there are Forms, this failure is not to be assimilated to sheer stupidity ... It is a failure to *see* that knowledge is not limited to our everyday experience and interests ... but requires thinking on our part and following through concepts that are not grasped adequately on the basis of our experience alone. (Annas 1981: 239)

This account of the division between the world of appearance and the world of ideas has a considerable impact on the way in which sexuality and death are understood in Platonic thought. Indeed, when Plato reflects on these two aspects of human life he instigates a movement away from their physical realities to what might be considered a spiritualizing of both. The sex drive is sublimated into the account that he gives of love and birth, while death is seen, not as that which destroys the self, but as that which liberates us from our physical prison. Such a move may be eminently reasonable: after all, the idea that life ends in death should, at the very least, make one pause for thought. Plato suggests that it is only by rejecting this transient world and accepting a transcendent reality that one is able to live a meaningful life.

Two texts, in particular, exemplify this trend towards the transcendent: *The Symposium* and *Phaedo*. The first is set at a dinner party, where each guest (including Socrates) offers a speech in praise of love. The second describes the death of Socrates, and involves a detailed discussion of the nature of death and the efficacy of Socratic proofs for the immortality of the soul.

The Symposium

Walter Hamilton makes an explicit connection between the intellectual arguments of *The Republic* and the purpose ascribed to love detailed in *The Symposium*: the philosopher, he argues, is to exhibit the traits of both wise man and lover (Plato 1951: 21). I would go further: it is the connection made between intellectual argument and the specific formulation of the nature of love that defines the Platonic move away from the physical to the ideal.

'Man'[2] is described in Platonic thought as a creature connected to two worlds: the immediate physical realm and the eternal world of the Forms. The question Plato addresses is how such a creature should live. The answer offered is that the ideal realm should form the focus for human life, and that this will necessitate a particular approach to love. While the structure of *The Symposium* is not simplistic (a plethora of voices are heard offering different views of love), the diverse arguments offered by the participants are bound together by a common theme: just as human life consists of a duality of physical and spiritual, so love must be understood as capable of assuming both these forms. Pausanius' description of love pre-empts that given by Socrates. He argues that there are two kinds of love, both emanating from Aphrodite, the goddess of love. The first is associated with 'the Common Aphrodite' (Plato 1951: 46; 181a) and involves simply the physical act of sex. Pausanius includes both hetero- and homosexual forms of love in this category, but his focus is clearly upon the physical expression and satisfaction of desire. The second form of love is associated with 'the Heavenly Aphrodite' and involves the rejection of the female in favour of (male) homosexual love. As Pausanius puts it, this kind of love has 'no female strain in her, but springs entirely from the male' (1951: 46–7; 182a). 'Sameness' becomes the quality that should attract the Platonic lover; 'the other', even in this context, is to be avoided (cf. Irigaray 1985a: 263, 323). Sexual expression of such a love is not so important: what matters is the desire for 'a lasting attachment and a partnership for life' (Plato 1951: 47; 182a). Socrates has yet to speak, and already a clear distinction is being made between physical and spiritual love, the latter being considered far superior to the former. Whether such an absolute distinction can be maintained is debatable, and, as we shall see, there are elements in the Dialogues that suggest a more complex relationship between the two realms.

The duality implied in Pausanius' speech is rendered explicit by Socrates. In his speech, sexual desire is apparently rejected in favour of a sublime form of love. Socrates presents both love and procreation as capable of being understood in terms of the physical and the spiritual, and, as with Pausanius before him, seeks to show the inferiority of physical love and the primacy of spiritual love.

Socrates locates his discussion of love in the words of the woman whom he acknowledges as his teacher, Diotima of Mantinea. Whether such a woman ever existed,[3] or whether she fulfils some darker purpose,[4] what matters here is that Diotima's words cohere with Plato's philosophy.[5] There is an ambivalence towards the nature of love which means it can be associated neither exclusively with the good and the beautiful, nor with the bad and the ugly: rather it lies somewhere between the two (Plato 1951: 80; 202a). Socrates' intention is to show how the power of love can be utilized to obtain a vision of the Forms of the Beautiful and the Good only if it is effectively idealized or spiritualized. Thus Socrates is required to show physical love to be inferior to spiritual love. However, by implying that physical love can be employed to progress to the spiritual/ideal, he suggests a deeper, more complex account of the relationship between his two realms: it is not possible simply to reject the physical in favour of the spiritual, for the two realms are connected.

Diotima distinguishes between the two forms of love in two ways. Firstly, she describes two types of creativity, both in terms of 'procreation'. One form involves the physical procreation of human children, the other the spiritual creation of various (higher) goods (Plato 1951: 86; 205b). She argues that both forms are concerned with achieving immortality (1951: 87; 207b); yet only one form (the spiritual) is capable of achieving this end. So the desire for children emanates from the desire that one's line might continue after one's death, giving one a kind of immortality. But the implication is that this kind of immortality is illusory, simply perpetuating the physical that is always a prey to death. Diotima contrasts such immortality, secured through physical offspring, with the kind of progeny that she suggests are far superior: the children of the soul, described as 'wisdom and virtue' (1951: 90; 209a). Such children are far preferable to human offspring, Diotima argues, for they are truly immortal. In this way, the exclusive female act of birthing is appropriated by the (male) philosopher: 'The pregnant, birth-giving male, like the male who practices midwifery, stands as the emblematic figure of true philosophy' (Cavarero 1995: 92).

Indeed, physical birthing is considered less significant than its intellectual counterpart, and is connected, fundamentally, with death. Centuries later this idea resonates in Samuel Beckett's affecting image of the human condition: '[Women] give birth astride a grave, the light gleams an instant, then it's night once more' (Beckett 1990: 83). The rejection of physical birth in favour of Socratic birthing leads to the denigration of physical experience. The world and its processes are seen as inferior to the heavenly world of Forms or Ideas. Paradoxically, 'the lifeless world of the Forms gives eternal life, the living world of nature is called a tomb' (Plumwood 1993: 97). What we have here is a philosophy that could be described as dependent upon resolving a kind of 'womb-envy' (Cavarero 1995: 103) by rejecting the physical *hystera* that the philosopher does not have in favour of a spiritual womb that the male can possess.

If the act of physical procreation is downgraded, so, it seems, is physical love. Diotima argues that love can be used to attain the Good, but only if it is distanced from its physical expression. So, just as love of women is associated purely with (inferior) procreation, so sexual intercourse is ultimately rejected as an inappropriate expression of love for the philosopher.[6] Diotima moves her listener through a succession of forms of love that are to be put aside if the philosopher is to attain the highest form of love. Love of boys opens the eyes to the contemplation of physical beauty. This leads to the recognition that beauty is not simply to be found in one but can be found in many. With this revelation, 'the intensity of his passion for one particular person' (Plato 1951: 92; 210b) will be relaxed, and he will realize that 'such a passion is beneath him and of small account' (1951: 92; 210b). Next, he will come to recognize the beauty of the soul to be of more value than the beauty of the body, and, when he encounters such beauty in another (man), will seek a companionship which is based upon a mutual desire for the beautiful. However this beauty is not like earthly examples of the beautiful, which, like earthly life, is 'never eternal, but is by nature changing, transient, temporary' (Cavarero 1995: 99). Rather, this beauty is revealed to be eternal, unchanging and absolute (Plato 1951: 93–4; 211a): in other words, the philosopher has arrived at the Form of Beauty that transcends the meagre examples found in this flawed world.

It is interesting to note the ambiguity that surrounds the idea of love in Platonic thought. On the one hand, such an account seems to negate the significance of the physical world, and particularly of women, who are irrevocably connected with physical procreation, associated with the lower life, and thus to be resisted. On the other, there is the sense that love, rightly expressed as the love between two equal men, can lead to the higher life. This suggests a more complex relationship between the two realms, although, even in this case, physical sexual expression is to give way to an ideal appreciation of the Forms.[7]

The problematizing of existence along gendered lines is given further expression in Aristophanes' speech. Aristophanes begins by linking the female with the earth, the male with the sun (Plato 1951: 59–60; 190b) – significant analogies when one considers the Platonic image of the Good as the Sun (*Republic* VI, 507–8) and the escape from the Cave which is set deep in the earth (*Republic,* VI, 514). Given this imagery, it is not surprising that the female and the kind of procreation dependent upon the female should be rejected as appropriate ways of ascending to the world of Forms, for 'the womb has been played with, made metaphor and mockery of by men' (Irigaray 1985a: 263). Indeed, Aristophanes goes further. His myth of the first humans describes these beings as composite circular entities, made up of a duality of organs and limbs. They are separated by Zeus as punishment for their overreaching hubris, and consequently spend their lives seeking their 'other half' (Plato 1951: 59–62; 190b–191e). These composite beings were of three kinds: female, male and hermaphrodite. According to Aristophanes, the hermaphrodites include 'lovers of women'. He adds that: 'most adulterers come from this class, as do women who are mad about men and sexually promiscuous' (1951: 62; 191d–e). By way of contrast, the halves of the male beings pursue only males: these are 'the best of their generation, because they are the most manly' (1951: 62; 192a). It could be argued that Aristophanes is not Socrates, or indeed Plato. But that which is implicit in Socrates' argument is made explicit in Aristophanes' argument: the female is irrevocably connected with the lower, physical life, while the male has the possibility of breaking free of the earth and ascending to the ideal world of the Forms.

It is difficult not to read Plato and get something of the sense that the physical world (and, in this case, physical love) is problematic, something to be derided. Erotic love, it seems, is lowly and potentially dangerous, something which has to be held in its rightful place if it is not to plunge one into the world of appearance and transience. At one point, Socrates describes the physical beauty of this world as 'a mass of perishable rubbish' (1951: 95; 212c) in comparison with ideal Beauty. This world, it seems, is a poor relation to the world of Forms.

While it is this picture of the relationship between the ideal and the physical that prevails in Platonic thought, a counter-trend can be identified which suggests a closer relationship between these polarized opposites. *Phaedrus* begins with Socrates praising the beauty of the spot where this dialogue on the nature of rhetoric will take place (Plato 1973: 25; 230b). Socrates goes so far as to argue that 'the place is sacred to Achelous', the river god, because the water is so cool for the feet. Despite this celebration of the physical as vehicle for the divine, Socrates moves on quickly to say, 'the fields and trees won't teach me anything' (1973: 26; 230d). Such a swift rebuttal suggests that the pull of the physical and its tangible beauty needs to be resisted if one is not to be subsumed in the world of appearance.

A similarly complex relationship between the worlds surfaces in the character of Alcibiades, who appears towards the end of *The Symposium* (Plato 1951: 100–11; 214e–222c). Alcibiades entertains the group with his account of his abortive attempt to seduce Socrates. While this could be read as an example of the difference between Socratic love and sexual intercourse, a different reading might be possible. Alcibiades has fallen in love with Socrates' intellect, and thus wants to love him physically. It is not Socrates' beauty (he was notoriously ugly) that has attracted him, but his ideas. And Socrates does not rebuff Alcibiades; rather he hopes that, given time, Alcibiades will move on from infatuation to the higher form of love.[8]

Both examples suggest a complex relationship between the physical and the spiritual. Despite appearances, it is not simply the case that Plato makes an outright rejection of the physical. And indeed, when thinking of the nature of love, we need to consider what an appropriate form of love is. As we shall see when we consider the ideas of the Marquis de Sade, to base love simply in the physical act of sex may lead to a disturbing and damaging account of human relationship.[9] The more ambiguous passages in Plato's work suggest that it might be possible to hold together both spiritual *and* physical forms of love. A transcendent option, grounded in the physical, might be a possibility.[10]

Phaedo

If *The Symposium* maps the Platonic movement away from the physical towards the ideal in relation to love, the dialogue of *Phaedo* focuses on the logical outcome of such a philosophy: death is not drawn as the end of life, but is idealized as the way of escaping the hindrance of the flesh. Val Plumwood's depiction of Plato's philosophy as a 'philosophy of death' (Plumwood 1993: 69) may be apt, but makes sense only if one understands the radical reversal of the values ascribed to birth and death in ordinary, 'unenlightened' life. If *The Symposium* portrays birth as leading inexorably to death, *Phaedo* portrays death as the way to life.

A large part of this dialogue is concerned with advancing arguments designed to establish the pre-eminence of the soul in comparison to the body. These are given more weight by the context in which they are rehearsed: Socrates is about to drink hemlock to effect the death sentence that has been passed against him. Once these arguments have been accepted, death will be revealed as something that should not be feared, but welcomed. Death moves from being the event that destroys us to that which simply marks 'the separation of the soul from the body' (Plato 1993: 9; 64c); it marks the '*untying* of the soul from the body that leads the soul back to its original home' (Cavarero 1995: 23). And if we accept that the soul is the essential self, the removal of the body need not frighten us, for 'we' will survive, even if the body does not.

Indeed, Plato goes further. It is not simply that death should not be feared: it is to be welcomed, for the body is an 'evil' (Plato 1993: 12; 66b) that hinders the life of the mind. Death thus constitutes an escape from the prison that is the body (1993: 13; 66d). Yet it is not simply a prison, an image that might at least suggest a connection with life; in *Phaedrus*, the body is linked explicitly with death. In striking language, Plato writes that it is a 'walking sepulchre which we call a body, to which we are bound like an oyster to its shell' (Plato 1973: 57; 250c). If *The Symposium* closes with the claim that the natural world is 'a dump' (Plumwood 1993: 69), *Phaedo* suggests that the body mirrors the prison (tomb?) of the cave so carefully detailed in *The Republic*.

Plato's response to this situation is to instigate a radical therapy. Philosophy, he has Socrates argue, is the practice of death in life (Plato 1993: 9; 64a), and ascetic discipline lies at its heart: the pleasures of food, drink and sex are all to be rejected (1993: 10; 64d). This statement may come as something of a surprise, given the setting of *The Symposium* at a rather raucous dinner party, where wine flows freely and there is much discussion of the way in which sex might be used to progress to the 'higher' forms of love.[11] Here a less optimistic note is, perhaps not surprisingly, placed upon carousing and feasting. In the face of death a different argument is advanced: by resisting those things that the body craves, the philosopher imposes a distance between soul and body (1993: 12; 66a). To anticipate death in life means that, when death itself comes, it will be welcomed as liberation (1993: 9; 64a). Indeed, any other response on the part of the philosopher would be absurd if they have genuinely cultivated the practice of dying to the body in this life (1993: 14; 67e).

The understanding of philosophy as the practice of death is the logical conclusion to the two worlds philosophy advanced in *The Republic*. Again, the physical world is rejected in favour of the transcendent world of Forms. Woman is further linked to the physical world, and twice in *Phaedo* the 'absurdity' of grief in the face of death is exemplified by women or by allusion to them. Xanthippe, Socrates' wife, is removed from the scene so that her crying will not disturb the tranquillity of the philosopher as he faces his death (1993: 3–4; 60a). Later, as Socrates drinks the hemlock, some of his friends begin to cry. His response is forthright:

> What a way to behave, my strange friends! Why, it was mainly for that reason that I sent the women away, so that they shouldn't make this sort of trouble; in fact, I've heard one should die in silence. Come now, calm yourselves and have strength. (1993: 78; 117d–e)

Woman, linked with the physical world, the cave, and this-worldly procreation is shown grieving for the loss of life. But the true (male) philosopher recognizes death not as the end of life but as the gateway to a fuller existence. No tears are necessary to greet death, for this world is a vale of tears to which death brings a fitting and liberating end. Indeed, only a woman could value this world – described as a rubbish heap of corruption (1993: 69; 110a) – above the glories of the real world that transcends it. Luce Irigaray expresses a sense of bewilderment that such a worldview could come to dominate Western conceptions of the human relationship with the natural world: 'What could induce anyone to choose as the more visible, the more true, and ultimately the more valuable something which is merely named and that is intended to replace something else that has charmed your whole life?' (Irigaray 1985a: 271).

On the face of it, this is a powerful and profound statement. But, given the nature and extent of human tragedy, I am not so sure that this dualistic response may not be rather reasonable.[12] Remember the context for *Phaedo*: the execution of a man whose only crime was to *make people think*. In such a world, the desire for a less arbitrary criterion of value is attractive. This does not mean that it is an accurate response; simply that it makes sense. The human challenge is to find a way of living in this world that makes sense of the suffering and pain to be found within it. Plato's answer is to posit a transcendent realm where there is no grief, pain or agitation. And, despite the many twists and turns of philosophy since, this desire for some kind of transcendent option remains. In his philosophy we see the beginnings of the Western desire to distance the human self from the natural world. We are travellers in a strange land, 'orphans of a simple, pure – and ideal – origin' (Irigaray 1985a: 293), who have become trapped in the physical world. This 'existential homelessness' (Plumwood 1993: 71) is felt in different ways in different parts of the Western tradition. In Platonic dualism it takes the form of rejecting this tangible, physical world in favour of belief in a world that transcends it. Philosophy, rather than arriving at conclusions gleaned from reflection upon the physical world, becomes concerned with metaphysics and what lies beyond/behind the physical in a hypothetical other world. Philosophy is thus the movement away from ignorance of what is not immediately comprehensible towards that which can be shown to exist beyond this human realm. If in Platonic philosophy the commitment to physical life, sexual love and reproduction is located in ignorance of the Forms, in Christian theology a further move is made. Sex becomes associated with sin, and, as a consequence, with the wages of sin, death.

Sin, sex and death in Augustine

Augustine is often credited with connecting Christian theology with the philosophies of Plato and Aristotle. Indeed, it is Plato's philosophy with which he particularly engages (cf. *City of God*, VIII, 5 and 12) and, although he is critical of certain aspects of Platonism, he is also at times fulsome in his praise. The Platonists are, he claims at one point, 'the noblest of all the philosophers' (Augustine 1998: 390; *City of God*, X, 1). Given such statements, it is perhaps not surprising that similarities can be found between the attitudes to sex and death present in Plato's work, and the way in which Augustine approaches these key features of human life. There is, however, a significant difference: Augustine's understanding of the nature of both sex and death takes place against the backdrop of his discussion of sin. According to Augustine, all human beings share in the fallen state precipitated by the actions of Adam and Eve. If death is the punishment for their disobedience, sexual intercourse is peculiarly affected by that mortality.

Such connections have led to what amounts almost to an orthodox position among critics regarding Augustine's responsibility for the sexual pessimism to be found in Christianity in particular and the Western tradition in general. He is, according to Ranke-Heinemann, 'the man who fused Christianity together with hatred of sex and pleasure' (Ranke-Heinemann 1991: 75). There is good evidence for such a claim; yet I shall argue against a straightforward connection between sex and death in Augustine's writings. What drives Augustine's theology/anthropology is less a hatred of pleasure, and more a desire to avoid the loss (and resulting pain) of valuing temporal, sensual things.[13] To commit oneself to such transient pleasures is to court death, and Augustine's theology, like Plato's philosophy, is driven by the desire to transcend this mutable, physical world. Far from being a perverse reaction to the facts of human existence, this seems an understandable response to the tragedy of human life, especially when one considers the way in which Augustine's theology is shaped by his own experience of loss and death. The question, of course, is whether such a bleak view of human life is the only one open to us if we accept the mutability of existence. Before we can consider alternative approaches to the facts of human existence, it is important to engage with Augustine, for the way in which he understands sex and death, and the relationship between the two, has had considerable ramifications for Western attempts to shape the spiritual life.

Problematizing the sensual

The Fall: defining sin   Crucial to Augustine's theology are his reflections upon the story of the Fall (Genesis 1–3), a story which he uses to shape his understanding of the human condition. According to Augustine, the story of Adam and Eve presents us with the vision of a humanity lost in sin. His definition of sin focuses on the primeval act of disobedience instigated by our primeval parents. In disobeying God, Adam and Eve lost paradise, and all humanity, as their heirs, shares in this loss. Because they disobeyed God, humanity is condemned to live 'as the beasts do, subject to death: the slave of his own lust, destined to suffer eternal punishment after death' (*City of God*, XII, 22; Augustine 1998: 533). Already we get a sense of the way in which the Fall perverts the prelapsarian nature of humanity. After this pivotal event, human beings are subject to the same laws as the animals, who must reproduce through sexual intercourse and who are destined to die. In describing sex and death as in some sense 'unnatural', Augustine develops what will become the orthodox Christian position. In contrast to those branded as heretics, who saw sex and death as part of the divinely ordained nature of things, Augustine sees both features as resulting from human sin (*Contra Julianum* 3, 6). For Pelagius (c.354–after 418), death is part of the nature of God's world. For Julian (386–454), sex and death were, from the very beginning, features of human life.

The sense that human life is linked with animal existence because of the Fall permeates Augustine's understanding of the nature of sin. The loss of their immortal nature is not the only punishment for their act of disobedience: through this act of rebellion, humanity has lost the ability to control what Augustine calls the 'shameful' parts of the body, viz., the sexual organs. There is a poetic form of justice here: disobedience towards God, whom they should have obeyed, is mirrored in the way in which the flesh that should obey their will is now outside of that control. God's judgement is immediate: as they experience 'a new stirring of their flesh', so they need to cover their nakedness (*City of*

God, XIII, 13; Augustine 1998: 555). This loss of control over unruly flesh leads Augustine to conclude that fallen human existence will be defined by conflict within the self. The flesh lusts against the spirit (a phrase used repeatedly), and it is from this conflict that we are born. Adam and Eve's disobedience is 'the origin of death in us, and we bear in our members, and in our vitiated nature, the striving of the flesh, or, indeed, its victory' (*City of God*, XIII, 13; 1998: 555).[14] Sex and death are thus viewed as punishments for the primal sin. Sex is identified with the unruly, animal body that defies the controlling power of the spirit; death pervades all human existence, turning life into its opposite (*City of God*, XIII, 10 and 11), and corrupting the original beauty of the physical body.

It is the loss of control over the body that for Augustine exemplifies the problematic experience of being human. Shame is an appropriate emotion to have when contemplating our sexual natures, for we are no longer in a position to control our desire (*City of God*, XIII, 24; 1998: 580). Lust and death are both punishments for sin, for through both we lose the control (or freedom) which was given to our primeval parents. The tragedy of the human condition is that it need not have been like this, for 'the corruption of the body, which presseth down the soul, was not the cause of the first sin, but its punishment; nor was it corruptible flesh that made the soul sinful, but the sinful soul that made the flesh corruptible' (*City of God*, XIV, 3; 1998: 585). This is a significant statement that undercuts any claim that Augustine sees the flesh as ultimately sinful. What is sinful is the *will* that disobeys God; but even the will can never be wholly evil. 'Evil' is always dependent upon the good for its existence (*City of God*, XI, 22) – an important clarification which shows Augustine's resistance to the Manichaean claim that the physical is intrinsically evil (cf. *Confessions*, XIII, 30). For Augustine, once a member of this sect, the flesh is not evil, and this implies a less negative account of the body than is sometimes suggested to be the case when considering Augustinian anthropology.[15]

Despite such clarifications, an almost unyielding pessimism informs Augustine's writing on the human condition. Both sex and death affect the loss of the image of God, which he locates in the mind (cf. *On the Trinity*, Book XII). In the act of sexual intercourse, the god-like capacity to reason is lost, and Augustine seems particularly concerned with the effect of the male orgasm when considering this phenomenon: 'when he achieves his climax, the alertness and, so to speak, vigilance of a man's mind is almost entirely overwhelmed' (*City of God*, XIV, 16; Augustine 1998: 614). Similarly, the universality of death reveals the loss of the immortality that the first human beings shared with God. Natural, unredeemed human life is nothing but 'a progression towards death' (*City of God* XIII, 10; 1998: 550). The connection between sex and death is similarly clarified in *The Good of Marriage*, where Augustine claims that only after the Fall is sexual intercourse possible, for it 'can only take place between mortal bodies' (*De bono coniugali*, 2; Augustine 2001a: 3). Presumably there would have been no sexual intercourse in Eden, although in practice Augustine's response to this question is ambiguous.

There is a further, more intimate connection between sex and death. Through sexual intercourse, the original sin of our primeval parents is passed on to each and every human being (cf. *City of God*, XIII, 23; 1998: 573; see also *On Marriage and Concupiscence*, Book I, chapter 13). No one is innocent. The womb is symbolized as the locus for death, and even the womb of Mary, the mother of Christ, is likened to a tomb from which Christ had to escape (Power 1995: 180). Sin is universal, and all stand in need of redemption. Only Christ, born of a virgin mother, is able to escape the universality of sin. In a shift that resonates with Platonic philosophy, birth is associated with death, while death is seen as releasing us from this life.

Consideration of Augustine's theory of sin leaves one with the sense that humanity is trapped in a dark, threatening, decaying universe. If anything, reflection on Augustine's theology illuminates the more positive aspects of Plato's thought on the role of the natural world. At least Plato suggests that one can use the physical to progress to the spiritual. For Augustine, the only hope is that God will send a redeemer, and this has been done in the person of Christ. What would lead someone to such an alienating and alienated vision of the physical world – which is, after all, our home? Augustine is almost unique among theologians for leaving a record of the psychology and experiences that would lead to such formularizing. His reflections upon his spiritual journey suggest important reasons for such an account.

Augustine's Confessions: experience and theology

> I lived in misery, like every man whose soul is tethered by the love of things that cannot last and then is agonized to lose them. (*Confessions*, IV, 6; Augustine 1961: 77)

Augustine's view of natural human life is one of unremitting misery. He is particularly concerned to show the emptiness of the sensual life in comparison to the fullness of the redeemed life. In the *Confessions*, Augustine uses his own experiences prior to his conversion to illustrate graphically this dichotomy between the old and new lives. In a work that has been seen as the first autobiographical text, he gives an account of his early life in which he pictures himself as one consumed by the sensual. It is from this perilous situation that he has been saved by Christ. It is not simply that he was subsumed in the natural by the pull of sexual desire; there is also a sense that, because he gave in to his desires, he submitted himself to the death that is punishment for the Fall.

Augustine describes his overwhelming desire to be loved as the driving force of his early years. This desire to 'love and be loved' (*Confessions*, II, 2; 1961: 43) seeks satisfaction through physical expression, and the language which he uses suggests that subsuming oneself in the desires of the body is tantamount to throwing oneself into the swamp-like clutches of the natural world:

> Bodily desire, like a morass, and adolescent sex welling up within me exuded mists which clouded over and obscured my heart, so that I could not distinguish the clear light of true love from the murk of lust. Love and lust together seethed within me. In my tender youth they swept me away over the precipice of my body's appetites and plunged me in the whirlpool of sin. (*Confessions*, II, 2; 1961: 43)

The language that Augustine uses elsewhere is similarly powerful, and suggests that he was out of control: 'I *ran wild* with lust' (Augustine 1961: 43; my emphasis); 'I allowed myself to be *carried away* by the sweep of the tide' (1961: 44; my emphasis); 'frenzy gripped me' (1961: 44). The sense that he views himself as a prey to base nature, thus losing his higher self, is reiterated. And this baser nature is identified with sexual desire.[16]

Indeed, sex is seen as something that not only defiles but also traps the unwary. There are hints that the all-encompassing nature of Augustine's desire finds expression in a variety of sexual experiments.[17] Ultimately, it leads to the relationship with the unnamed 'concubine' with whom Augustine lived for around fifteen years, and with whom he fathered a child. Augustine describes this experience in less than positive terms: 'I also fell in love, which was a snare of my own choosing' (Augustine 1961: 55). The image of being trapped in the sensual realm is repeated: he talks of the 'bonds of woman's love' (Augustine 1961: 158), a description reiterated elsewhere when writing of those who 'bind themselves in the chains of marriage' (*De sancta uirginitate*, 16; Augustine 2001b: 83). This image dominates his account of sexual relationships, both licit and illicit. Sex plays a particular role in linking us more strongly to the things of this world, thus losing our connection with the transcendent things of the divine: 'The depths to which we sink . . . They are our passions, our loves, the unclean leanings of our own spirits, which drag us downward in our love of the world and its cares' (*Confessions* XIII, 7; 1961: 315).

It is difficult to decide how seriously one should take Augustine's posturing when he details the overriding nature of his promiscuity. For example, when he talks of his concubine, it is difficult to discern the full extent of his feelings for her. Initially, he claims that there was 'no special reason' for his choosing her; he simply needed an object for his lust. Yet he then comments that 'she was the only one and I was faithful to her' (*Confessions*, IV, 2; 1961: 72). This suggests a much deeper relationship than the superficial one at which he hints. Such a monogamous relationship seems a strange fruit of such overpowering sexual desires.

Be that as it may: Augustine is concerned to show that his conversion to Christianity put an end to the power which lust had over him. The biblical passage that he reads after hearing the voice telling him to 'Take up and read' is particularly significant for challenging his attitude towards sex: 'Not in revelling and drunkenness, not in lust and wantonness, not in quarrels and rivalries. Rather arm yourselves with the Lord Jesus Christ; spend no more thought on nature and nature's appetites' (Romans 13: 13, 14; *Confessions* VIII, 12; 1961:178). It is this distinction between sexual desire and spiritual discipline that shapes the material of the *Confessions* and his account of the spiritual life. Having said that, sex is only one aspect of the problem with which Augustine grapples. Ultimately his concern lies with addressing the problem of mortality in its widest sense. He asks whether it is possible to be 'blessed and mortal' (Augustine 1998: 376). Is it possible to live the good life while in this flesh which is a prey to death? When he writes of mortality he has in mind both the pull of the physical life (particularly sexual desire) and the reality of loss occasioned by death. Elsewhere, he will argue that it is not possible to be both blessed and mortal, for 'all men must necessarily be miserable while they are mortal' (Augustine 1998: 377). Only the promise of an immortal life brings hope.

There is, however, a degree of tension in Augustine's thought at this point. Human life might be wrought by the conflict between flesh and spirit; mortality might bring with it the misery of eventual death; yet the world is beautiful because God made it (Augustine 1961: 329). At times he even seems to contradict his initial claims that without God's explicit revelation there can be no hope. He seems to accept the claims of the neo-Platonist Plotinus that it is possible to infer from the beauty of the transient and temporal to the eternal beauty of the divine (*City of God*, X, 14).[18] Similarly, he can look with wonder upon being human, writing that: 'For man himself is a greater miracle than any miracle performed by man' (*City of God*, X, 13; 1998: 411). Yet it is the struggle between flesh and spirit to which he continually returns, and this conflict evidently expresses the struggle going on within Augustine. In seeking a resolution to this struggle, he arrives at two strategies: firstly, his desires are sublimated into the concept of God, and, secondly, he focuses on the need for order and control as the values necessary for living the spiritual life.

Solving the problem

The sublimation of desire: Augustine's concept of God   In her fascinating study of Augustine's relationships with women, Kim Power employs a psychoanalytic framework to argue that Augustine's theology reflects a particular way of coping with the experience of loss known as cognitive dissonance (Power 1995: 101–7). While not employing such a technical framework, I shall argue that it is possible to understand Augustine's concept of God only if it is seen to mirror the sexual desires which shaped his earlier life. The catalyst for the sublimation of such desires into the concept of God is the reality of loss experienced early on in Augustine's life. Two specific losses are referred to in the *Confessions*: the loss of a close friend and the loss of his concubine. The first arises from an unstoppable natural force (death), while the second is partly Augustine's responsibility: his woman is sent away (apparently by his mother Monica) in order to facilitate an advantageous marriage. The power of the language that Augustine uses to describe these losses says much about the effect they had upon him. In the case of his friend, his grief affects the very way in which he experiences life in this world. He feels alienated from everything: 'My own country became a torment and my own home a grotesque abode

of misery.' The world becomes a miserable place, and Augustine recalls how he 'hated all the places we had known together' (*Confessions*, IV, 4; 1961: 76). In the case of his lover, a more complex series
of emotions come into play, possibly because Augustine is aware of
his own responsibility for this loss; perhaps things did not need to be
like this: 'At first the pain was sharp and searing, but then the wound
began to fester, and though the pain was duller there was all the less
hope of a cure' (*Confessions*, VI, 15; 1961: 131).

What seems to abide from both experiences is a persistent sense of
the fragility of life and relationship. It is a theme to be found throughout his writings: 'the more friends we have, and the more places we
have them in, the further and more widely do we fear that some evil
may befall them out of all the mass of the evils of this world' (*City of
God*, XIX, 8; 1998: 929). The anxiety one feels for one's loved ones
cannot be attributed simply to paranoia: as Peter Brown points out,
throughout his life Augustine was to experience the death of several
close friends (Brown 1969, 2000). Opening oneself up to intimacy
makes one vulnerable to losses of this kind. These experiences are
reflected in his theology, and, as Kim Power notes, his familiarity with
loss leads to an understanding of love that connects it with pain, just
as sex is linked with death:

> His sexual experience put him intimately in touch with the archetypal
> connections between sexuality and mortality. These he wove into a com-
> plex theology of sexual desire as the symbol of death. (Power 1995:
> 128)

In response to such events, Augustine seeks a love that is not open to
this kind of change, a love that does not involve the possibility of loss
and the accompanying pain. Even when he finds this invulnerable love
in the heart of God, it does not lessen his desire for human contact. He
is able to write, rather touchingly, of the significance and inevitability
of grief when friends die (Augustine 1998: 930). Despite resisting the
pull of the natural, human love is still a good for Augustine, even if it
is ultimately surpassed by the love of God.

Such reflections suggest something of a tension in Augustine's theology. With his conversion, Augustine's attitude towards the things of
this world, at least ostensibly, shifts: having thrown himself into the
mutable and changing world of human love, Augustine argues that
temporal things should be rejected as 'they do not last' (*Confessions*,

IV, 10; 1961: 80). His desire is for something which 'cannot perish' (*City of God*, XII, 8; Augustine 1998: 509), and he finds this in God.

Indeed, the connection between the experience of losing human friends and lovers and that of finding the eternal God is closely related. Reflecting upon his experiences prior to his conversion, Augustine feels that, as his misery deepened, God came closer (*Confessions*, VI, 16). Instead of being caught up in the transient beauty of earthly things, subject always to decay, he comes to perceive the eternal beauty of God, a beauty which is 'seen by the inner eye of the soul, not by the eye of the flesh' (*Confessions*, VI, 16; 1961: 132). This immutable love comes to displace the human love that previously held Augustine in its thrall. Human love is sublimated into divine love, although the words on friendship suggest that this cannot be consistently maintained. The sublimation of the sexual is perhaps more successful. When reflecting on what he loves when he loves God, he deliberately contrasts the qualities of the divine lover with 'the beauty of the natural order'. He does not see God's beauty with his eyes, hear his voice with his ears, or smell his sweetness with his nose. Tellingly, he does not appreciate the 'limbs such as the body delights to embrace' (*Confessions*, X, 6; 1961: 211). The superficiality of love based on sensory perception is replaced by the lasting love grounded in the inner self that knows the divine.

The goods of physical beauty that, one suspects, formed the basis for Augustine's sexual relationships are rejected, and human love comes to be spiritualized. There may be good reasons for seeking a love that is not based upon the transitory delights of physical appearance and sensation: one reason might be maturity. What is troubling is that Augustine rejects the possibility that one could have a mature relationship with a human lover; his desire is grounded exclusively in an eternal and transcendent divine lover. Not surprisingly, Augustine is similarly at pains to separate the physical from the spiritual: 'all nature is not God' (*City of God*, VI, 8; 1998: 255); 'in true theology . . . the earth is the work of God, not His mother' (*City of God*, VI, 8; 1998: 255).

Yet Augustine cannot completely avoid the pull of the sexual. He may resist it in his relationships, but his concept of God reveals a God described in overtly sexual terms. God is a jealous lover who views the over-ardent spouse as an adulteress 'committing fornication against the true God' (*On Marriage and Concupiscence*, Book I, chapter 5). Christ is the 'sole husband' (*De bono coniugali*, 32; 2001a: 59) to whom the Christian should submit. When Augustine describes the power of his love for God it resonates with the language of the ardent lover and gives an insight into Augustine's own sexual experience: 'You [God] shone upon me; your radiance enveloped me; you put my blindness to flight. You shed your fragrance about me; I drew breath and now I gasp for your sweet odour. I tasted you, and now I hunger and thirst for you. You touched me, and I am inflamed with love of your peace' (*Confessions*, X, 27; 1961: 232). In his human relationships, such overpowering love opened the way to the grief associated with loss. Now, sublimated into the divine, he can experience these emotions without fearing the loss of the lover/other.

Such passionate language seems somewhat incongruous when put alongside the rather distant God who emerges from Augustine's writings. In Book VII of the *Confessions*, Augustine paints a picture of a remote God who is incorruptible, immutable, immortal. Yet by applying such passionate language to this impassible God, Augustine succeeds in making love safe. This lover will never be lost; this friend will never die. Similarly, the advocacy of virginity as the model for the spiritual life operates alongside the attempt to take the unpredictability and vulnerability out of human relationships. God is given the role of lover for the virgin (*De sancta uirginitate*, 55), and his love is seen as preferable to the mutable, inconstant love of a human lover (*De sancta uirginitate*, 56).

Death is never very far away in Augustine's writings from the sublimation of desire. The vulnerability of the sexual/human relationship hints at the mortality of the human condition. The desire to find something that is not itself subject to loss permeates his theology. And, just as sexual desire is made safe in the concept of God, so the problem posed by mortality is sublimated into the idea that death operates as a gateway to eternal life.

Central to Augustine's theology is the belief that death is not the end, that there is an eternal life beyond this temporal existence (cf. *City of God*, I, 11) which constitutes the Christian hope. '"Life" will only be truly happy when it is eternal' (*City of God*, XIV, 25; 1998: 628). While resisting the Platonic notion that only the soul will survive death, Augustine paints a picture of the resurrection body as one quite different from the temporal body that we now inhabit. Such bodies 'will need no tree to guard them against death from sickness or old age, nor other corporeal food to protect them from any kind of hunger or thirst' (Augustine 1998: 569). The need for these things will be removed from spiritual bodies, and with the removal of need, so the possibility of loss, decay and death will also disappear. In similar vein, Augustine hopes for the transformation of desire in heaven. Bodily pleasure is seen as nothing compared to the joys of heaven (*Confessions*, IX, 10), and he anticipates the time when 'we shall enjoy each other's beauty without any lust' (Augustine 1998: 1164).

A tension emerges from all this. Augustine, like Plato, problematizes the physical. Yet by describing the rule of sin, he goes further: the physical can never lead to God. Sublimating love in the divine enables the possibility of an invulnerable love; yet at times he seems acutely aware of the dangers of making this move. He uses Virgil's myth of Cacus to criticize a life which seeks to make itself invulnerable to the chance and change of ordinary human existence (*City of God*, XIX, 12). Cacus was a fabulous monster that lived totally apart from human contact. All he desired was to be left alone, and in peace. Augustine notes that he has control over his members – a striking observation, given Augustine's comments that the bliss of Eden included control over the sexual organs. Only hunger disturbs Cacus' peace. In some ways, his seems to be the kind of life that Augustine espouses: yet, when he recounts this tale, he is critical of such a lifestyle. It is good to live in peace, but one should live in peace *with others*. But once one brings others into the equation it is difficult to see how one could live an invulnerable life. Moreover, by highlighting the importance of relationship, Augustine effectively challenges the idea that invulnerability might be a virtue. Love necessitates risk-taking; opening oneself to the other involves the possibility that one's love might be rejected, or that the lover might be taken by death. The God invulnerable to change would not be capable of such a relationship: although it is here that the crucified God of Christian theology hints at a different way of understanding the divine. The desire to be impassible may make sense as an immediate response to grief. But it is difficult – maybe even impossible – to imagine a love which does not include the possibility of loss. It may even be that the possibility of loss is what makes love so valuable in the first place. In shaping his account of the spiritual life, Augustine allows the desire for invulnerability full rein. His account of the changeless God leads to a spirituality defined by order and control.

Order and control: spiritual praxis in Augustine's theology
Augustine's vision of the spiritual life reflects many of the features applied to his concept of God. Augustine's concern is to detail how one should live as a Christian in this mutable world, and he argues

that the best way to do this is to instigate a proper order and control upon the things of the flesh. This is not simply a case of fixing upon an appropriate way of structuring the human social world: Augustine claims that the desire for order reflects God's will for the creation. All order comes from God (*City of God*, V, 11). If we are to be obedient to God, and thus resist the primal act of disobedience that led to the Fall, we must live properly ordered lives. This may prove difficult, given the stirrings of the flesh, but 'the peace of all things lies in the tranquillity of order', an order which Augustine describes as 'the disposition of equal and unequal things in such a way as to give to each its proper place' (*City of God*, XIX, 13; 1998: 938).

Living in such an ordered way has a social and personal focus that reflects the belief that a rightly ordered life will be based upon an acceptance of hierarchy. Socially, this means that Augustine will support the claims for male authority in church and home. As Power has shown, in part this social structure is based upon Augustine's gendered understanding of the mind. The faculty of the mind concerned with wisdom (*sapientia*) is defined in masculine terms, and is to subjugate the faculty of knowledge (*scientia*), which is defined in feminine terms and deals with the understanding of worldly things. Just as the mind should be properly ordered, so the mind should control the body. Both mind and body are created by God, but the mind is to rule the body if one is to live the kind of life God expects from his creatures. This is an important distinction, for it means that evil arises not from the flesh, but from the will that turns away from God. Augustine offers a graphic illustration of what he has in mind:

> Suppose there to be two men, similar in the temperament of their soul and body. Both of them see the beauty of another person's body; but one of them is moved to desire to enjoy it unlawfully, whereas the other remains steadfast in the chastity of his will. What, do we suppose, causes there to be an evil will in the one but not in the other? What produces it in the man in whom it is produced? Not the body's beauty, for that was exhibited to eyes of both, yet did not produce an evil will in both. (*City of God*, XII, 6; 1998: 506)

This suggests that Augustine will not go down the path of some of the patristic theologians who blame women for sexual sins of men.[19] If the mind controls the body, then the individual's will is at fault if it lusts after another.

Recognizing the role of the will goes some way to clarifying Augustine's account of virginity as the way of living the Christian life. In developing virginity as a form of spiritual praxis, Augustine, like other Christians of the period, builds upon classical notions of what this entails, but with significant differences. For Greeks and Romans, virginity was, on the whole, a transitory state which one adopted – in the case of women, prior to marriage, or, in the case of men, as a way of controlling one's life – and thus had its basis in medicine.[20] Alternatively, it might have a religious function, as in the case of the vestal virgins or the Delphic oracle.[21] Christian views of virginity moved away from this rather pragmatic approach. The Christian ideal of virginity arose, in part, from the desire to convince their contemporaries that they held high moral standards. Misunderstanding of the Christian ritual of the Eucharist had led to the idea that Christianity advocated loose morality. In advocating virginity, such a misunderstanding was refuted. At the same time, the account of virginity as a 'temporary' state was rejected: instead, it constituted a permanent commitment to a particular way of life.

Now, Augustine's account of virginity does not focus simply upon bodily integrity as defining the virgin/spiritual life. While he sees virginity as the way of living the spiritual life, he does not see bodily integrity as itself akin to holiness, for 'the holiness of the body does not lie in the integrity of its intimate parts, nor in the fact that they are not defiled by touch' (*City of God*, I, 18; 1998: 28). The important distinction is this: 'sanctity of body is not lost while sanctity of mind remains' (Augustine 1998: 28). Indeed, 'sanctity of body is ... lost when the sanctity of the mind is violated, even if the body remains intact' (Augustine 1998: 28). Such views explain the largely sympathetic approach he takes to the Christian virgins raped during the sack of Rome. The mind is the seat of virtue or sin,[22] and thus what matters is the state of one's mind, not, it would seem, the state of one's body. This emphasis on the importance of the mind may reflect a residual Manichaeism. For the Manichees, the flesh was unimportant, for it was part of the evil physical world. Thus sexual misdemeanours were relatively unimportant as they affected only the flesh. Augustine sees things differently. It is not that the flesh is evil; rather, the mind is (or, at least, *should be*) in control of the body.

It is unfortunate that this potentially positive message is sometimes lost. At times, Augustine seems to take his theory of the will to extremes, instigating what Graham Shaw might well describe as a form of 'Thought-Police' (Shaw 1987: 40–45). Augustine's claims that the famous – and to Roman eyes, honourable – Lucretia may have responded lustfully to her rape at the hands of Tarquinius Sextus (*City of God*, I, 19) seems to mitigate the horror of the crime, as if rape might not be rape if her body in some way responded. Responsibility (somewhat paradoxically, given Augustine's earlier comments) shifts from the perpetrator's actions to the victim's responses. Augustine is at pains to say that only she and God will know the truth of the matter, but it does suggest a rather ambiguous attitude to those who suffer such violations at the hands of others.

The body, then, seems to assume a rather neutral role in Augustine's ethics. Despite this, it is the most bodily of acts – sex – that tends to form the focus for Augustine's concern with structuring the appropriate Christian life. As we have seen, for Augustine, the Fall is the event through which humanity lost control over the body. Redemption, in part, involves initiating a degree of control over the flesh: hence the emphasis on virginity. Although other aspects of bodily existence are also discussed,[23] it is not difficult to see why sex will preoccupy Augustine as he works out his vision of the spiritual life.

Augustine's fixation on the problem of spontaneous erection clarifies the logic of this connection (*Confessions*, X, 30; *On Marriage and Concupiscence*, Book I, chapter 7; *City of God*, XIV, 16, 20, 23). As has been noted, the disobedience of the sexual organs to the rule of mind is viewed as one of the primary punishments for Adam and Eve's disobedience of God's command. In Eden, Augustine claims, the penis would have been subject to Adam's will (*City of God*, XIV, 23), a position which is reversed by the Fall. If sin is defined as disobedience, and the penis is characterized by its disobedience to the mind, it is relatively easy to conclude that sex is something sinful in itself.

The desire to return to the control over the erection possible in Eden haunts Augustine, and ultimately shapes the way in which the spiritual and the sexual are opposed in his theology. If one is to be spiritual, the sexual must be repressed. During his discussion of the need for clothes after the Fall, Augustine argues that this is principally to cover 'these offending members' which are no longer subject to the control of the mind (*On Marriage and Concupiscence*, Book I, chapter 7). 'Since shame arose from that which produced indecent pleasure', decency, it seems, might be retained if these organs are concealed (*On Marriage and Concupiscence*, pp. 105–6). This is all the more important, given that Augustine wistfully accepts that it will not always be possible to control the erection in this life: 'our wish ought to be nothing less than the non-existence of these desires, even if the accomplishment of such a wish be not possible in the body of this death' (*On Marriage and Concupiscence*, Book 1, Chapter 30; p. 128).[24] Sexual desire is thus connected with the curse of mortality. The important thing is to impose as much order as possible upon the unruly body, and thus, however imperfectly, to defy the bondage of death.

The desire to maintain some kind of order over sexuality has a particular impact upon his account of marriage. It should be noted that Augustine's ideas about marriage are considerably more positive than those offered by some of his contemporaries. For John Chrysostom (347–407), marriage was an unfortunate consequence of the Fall. Prior to this event, there was no sexual intercourse in Eden. One of the most disturbing consequences of Eve's disobedience was that it destroyed the idyll of virginity. In its stead arises marriage, conceived as a consequence of the curse. Augustine's views initially sound rather similar. Marriage is primarily viewed as a means for controlling rampant sexuality; it is necessary 'for those who lack self-control' (*De sancta uirginitate*, 21; 2001b: 93; see also *De bono coniugali*, 17). More positively, perhaps, it can be viewed as bringing a degree of good out of evil *if* it succeeds in imposing some kind of control on the sexual impulse (*On Marriage and Concupiscence*, Book I, chapter 8). Such control is connected, invariably, with procreation, which is the only appropriate reason for sexual intercourse. Augustine seems to suggest that, if rightly understood in this way, sex can be made subject to reason itself. Conversely, if a couple engage in sex purely for pleasure, then it 'is no longer subject to reason, but to lust' (*De bono coniugali*, 11; 2001a: 25).

This ambiguity gives a sense of the minefield that is Augustinian sexual ethics. Even when he writes of what he considers to be 'appropriate' sexual activity, Augustine is less than positive. Sexual intercourse leading to reproduction may be legitimate, but the *desire* to procreate is still a brute instinct, shared with beasts and birds (*De bono coniugali*, 22). Not surprisingly, perhaps, any claim that God willed sexual reproduction from the beginning is treated with a degree of scepticism. The divine command to 'increase and multiply' (Genesis 1:8), made prior to the Fall, is a metaphor for *spiritual* creativity, not sexual procreation, an interpretation which resonates with Plato's account of idealized birthing in *The Symposium*. Yet at times Augustine praises the fellowship of marriage, moving beyond those such as

Chrysostom who link it irrevocably with the Fall. 'The first natural link in human society is between man and wife' (*De bono coniugali* I; Augustine 2001a: 3); it is 'the natural compact . . . between the sexes' (*De bono coniugali*, 3; 2001a: 7). Despite such warm words, Augustine refuses the possibility that the sexual act, in the context of a loving relationship, might be self-authenticating. Talk of the importance of 'a rightly-ordered love' (*City of God*, XI, 16; 1998: 471) is located in the context of an argument that distinguishes reason from pleasure. Pleasure is always problematic, for invariably it effects the loss of the mind. The best solution to this problem is always abstinence, and while 'marriage and continence are two goods . . . the second is better' (*De bono coniugali*, 8; 2001a: 19). If one is a virgin, one can more easily ponder the eternal, unimpeded by the temporal things which can so easily dictate the experiences of the married (*De bono coniugali*, 13), and one gets the feeling that Augustine has in mind not simply the demands of running the home, but the demands – and delights – of the marital bed.

Spirituality is thus defined as the attempt to live the ordered and controlled life. Sex is problematic for it defies that kind of discipline, and thus bears witness to the continuing punishment for the Fall. It is difficult not to feel that Augustine's account of the spiritual arises from his own personal struggles.[25] At the very least, he appears to view his own sex life as one that refused to be controlled. Alongside this sense of chaos lies the experience of grief, and much of Augustine's spirituality revolves around the desire to gain a degree of freedom from loss and vulnerability. His focus on a transcendent God is mirrored in an account of the spiritual that seeks to distance it from the unpredictability of ordinary human existence. Yet the desire for intimacy remains. When Augustine offers idealized descriptions of intercourse in Eden, one feels something of his own desire for a sexual relationship that does not disturb his peace of mind. Paradise is the place where there is no sadness, nor, tellingly, any 'empty pleasure' (*City of God*, XIV, 26; 1998: 629). The prelapsarian relationship between Adam and Eve echoes Augustine's own, unspoken desire. Here, there is a 'faithful fellowship of honest love . . . between the pair; there is *concord and alertness of mind and body*, and God's commandment was kept without labour' (Augustine 1998: 629; my emphasis). In this ideal world, even intercourse would be devoid of the turbulence of lust, for 'the man would have poured his seed into his wife's womb in tranquillity of mind and without any corruption of her body's integrity' (Augustine 1998: 629).

Evidently this vision of the sexual act appeals to Augustine as it does not disrupt the will. There is no sense in which one might be swept up in the turmoil of passion. While such a desexualized account of human relationship might be safe, would it be fulfilling? The other/partner seems unreal and voiceless in this controlled and ordered universe. Augustine craves a relationship that is invulnerable to chance, change and loss: and, when drawing both his concept of God and of the spiritual life, it is this image that is forefront in his mind. But, as Martha Nussbaum has suggested in comments which will be taken up later in this work (Nussbaum 1990, ch. 5), is it possible – or indeed desirable – to construct one's values apart from the flux of human life? The desire to transcend the agony of transitory existence may make sense (especially when one reflects on Augustine's experience of loss), but to ground one's spirituality on an invulnerable transcendent may avoid a serious grappling with what it means to live in this mutable and changing world.

Conclusion: transcending the immanent: structuring meaning and spirituality

For both Plato and Augustine, the overriding issue confronting human beings lies with how one is to live a meaningful life in the face of death. For Plato, the answer exists in grasping the reality of the Forms, and living in the light of that transcendent possibility. For Augustine, living meaningfully requires living the properly ordered life. While Plato suggests that it is possible to use sexual desire as a way of moving towards the beauty of the Forms, provided one sees it as part of a transitional process, Augustine problematizes the sexual as that which defies order, thus excluding it from the spiritual life. This polarization of sexual and spiritual has shaped Western accounts of spirituality until relatively recently.

Despite the problems such a polarization has created, Augustine is clearly addressing an important issue. His refusal to allow any trivial response to the reality of human mortality is laudable. Death does stand at the end of all endeavour and experience, and throwing oneself into the sexual/sensual may not be the best way of dealing with this fact. Plato has Socrates say that 'the unexamined life is not worth living', and the idea that thought and contemplation open the way to how we should live has also shaped Western spirituality. Similarly,

Augustine resists the idea that throwing oneself into a meaningless, sensual existence will solve the problem of death: indeed it may make things worse by trivializing human relationship.[26] His criticisms of the Roman gods are important in this context, for he sees them as simply legitimating the lustful impulses of human beings: 'Human infirmity cannot be restrained from the perpetration of damnable deeds for as long as a seemingly divine authority is given to the imitation of such deeds' (*City of God*, IV, 1; 1998: 143). What remains to be seen is whether a more positive account of the sexual might be possible, grounded, perhaps, in the muted comments Plato makes on how sexuality might provide a gateway to the appropriate human life.

For Plato and Augustine, meaning is found in the life that transcends sex and the reality of death. My intention is to explore the possibility of a meaningful life based upon a fundamental acceptance of these elements as constitutive of our humanity. It may prove difficult to maintain an immanental spirituality without some revised form of transcendence, and the next chapter will suggest something of the difficulties of resisting a transcendental account of human being. Even secular philosophers who have deliberately rejected the notion of the transcendent God/Good have found such an account of human being hard to maintain, as we shall discover by considering the existentialist/humanist philosophies of Jean-Paul Sartre and Simone de Beauvoir.

2

Transcending the Void: Sex and Death in Sartre and Beauvoir's Existentialism

Introduction

Notions of transcendence are by no means limited to the religious account of the world offered by figures such as Augustine. If anything, the twentieth century was dominated even more by the desire to transcend the limits imposed upon humanity by mortality. Death remains problematic, hence the convoluted attempts to mask its reality. It is not simply that we live in an age that has little experience of those who are dying; it is more that death is treated as something accidental, an event which could be avoided and for which blame is always attributable.[1] Despite death's continuing status as the last taboo, religious solutions to the fear of death no longer seem credible in a secular society. This does not mean, however, that no connection has been made between sex and death. If we are mortal, we are mortals whose sexuality hints at the darkness and inevitability of death.

The aim of this chapter is to trace the development of a humanistic transcendental ethic in the work of the existentialist writers Jean-Paul Sartre and Simone de Beauvoir. Potentially, this offers some interesting insights for this study and explains why their ideas are placed after the engagement with Plato and Augustine. The rejection of a transcendent God by both suggests that it might be possible to reflect upon the meaning of sex and death in such a way that one need not find meaning by rejecting the importance of being mortal. Transcendence might be located in this world rather than in some hypothetical other-world. In this sense, both Augustine's transcendent God and Plato's transcendent Forms/Ideas are rejected. Indeed, it would seem that in the philosophies of both Sartre and Beauvoir it is precisely a *this-worldly* form of transcendence that is being advocated. The goal of humanity is to find a way of 'standing out' from this world (or 'ex-sisting') through one's endeavours. While locating humanity firmly in this world, and accepting the finality of death, mortality, however, remains problem-atic, for it suggests something of the absurdity of the human condi-tion. If death is to be overcome – principally by finding a way of transcending the processes of this world – the issue of human sexual-ity must also be confronted, and in practice this necessitates the denial of the female/feminine. In this sense, Sartrean existentialism, while providing some important insights into how transcendence might be redefined, will not escape the desire to transcend the physical world. Surprisingly, this philosophy can be shown to be not so different in its aspirations from those that drive the supposedly contrasting philoso-phies of Plato and Augustine.

Death in Sartrean existentialism

Defining human being: the role of consciousness

One of the key developments of existentialism lies in its challenge to the way in which prior philosophies and theologies have privileged notions of essence over existence. If for Plato the philosophical task was to determine the universal features of human being, for Sartre and Beauvoir the very enterprise of seeking an essentialist answer is re-jected. Instead, emphasis is placed upon the concrete, particular real-ity of existence, which is granted priority for all human questioning. So, 'man exists, turns up, appears on the scene, and, only afterwards, defines himself' (Sartre [1946] 1985: 15). Thus, any system of thought is grounded in the real-life experience of real individual existences. As Sartre put it, there is no blueprint for human existence that we follow; rather the peculiarly human task is to create our self. In this sense, there is no essential humanity; rather 'man will be what he will have planned to be' ([1946] 1985: 16). Beauvoir, applying this message to the lives of women, introduces an important element into the existentialist message: socialization has to be taken into account, and this leads to her famous conclusion that 'one is not born, but rather becomes, a woman' ([1949]1972: 296).

Such ideas suggest a radically different way of viewing human life from that discussed in the previous chapter. For Plato and Augustine, the meaningful human life is based upon an acceptance that meaning is to be found outside this world, in the Good/God. Yet, strangely, the desire for something that transcends this mortal life lives on within this peculiarly humanist ethic. In order to explore how this happens, it is necessary to consider the way in which consciousness forms the basis for the existentialist account of the self. In defining consciousness, the issue of transcendence comes to form the central category of Sartrean thought, and, by extension, influences Beauvoir's feminist development.

At the heart of Sartre's definition of consciousness lies a tacit acceptance of Cartesianism. Descartes' establishment of the conscious self in the *cogito* ('I think, therefore I am'), according to Sartre, expresses 'the absolute truth of consciousness becoming aware of itself' ([1946] 1985: 36). Similarly, this consciousness has a transcendent quality: man is 'constantly outside himself . . . it is by pursuing transcendent goals that he is able to exist' ([1946] 1985]: 50).

At the same time, Sartre's formulation of the nature of consciousness displays important differences. As Dilman notes, for Sartre consciousness is not an internal faculty or something distinct from the body (Dilman 1987: 64). There is a more complex relationship that involves a full acceptance of the physical being of humanity. In this sense, the potential for transcendence which Sartre ascribes to humanity is more akin to the transcendental quality of the mind, which enables one to transcend one's physical placing through intellectual pursuits, than it is to Plato's formulation of an immortal soul that can transcend existence in the body. At the same time, death remains problematic, for, if consciousness is not radically and ontologically distinct from the body, when the body dies, it will die.

Indeed, Iris Murdoch sees Sartre as decidedly 'unCartesian' in his rejection of the idea that consciousness could exist separately from physical activity, which lies at the heart of Descartes' account (Murdoch [1953] 1967: 62). Sartre's account, in contrast to Descartes' own, is phenomenological: consciousness is always consciousness *of* the world (Sartre [1971] 1999: 56). Such an insight is important, for it suggests the possibility of a form of transcendence to be found in this world, not simply imposed upon it from without. It might be possible to hold together the transcendent and the immanent in such a way that neither is allowed to dominate the other.

Yet the way in which Sartre develops this position is open to criticism on several fronts. The maintenance of the claim that human being is defined by consciousness can lead to an overly intellectual engagement with the realities of human life. When Sartre 'reflects' on the 'moral and political implications' of a highly publicized rape case (cf. Beauvoir [1981] 1985: 61), one wonders whether such reflections are really appropriate. Beauvoir recalls the context for this discussion. A Vietnamese student had been raped by a black immigrant, and Sartre is asked to write an article on this event for *Libération*. In her memoir, Beauvoir focuses on Sartre's struggle with the elements of the case, but she details less the contents of the article and more the everyday discussions and events that surrounded Sartre during the writing of this piece: so, Sartre drinking spiced tea, talking with his editor, and so on. There seems to be the sense that the socio-political lessons to be derived from such an event are more significant than the suffering of the girl herself, who remains nameless in Beauvoir's account. Life is seen through an intellectualist lens, rather than 'up close and personal'. This might enable important insights into the phenomenon of rape, but it might also render the girl herself silent, her experience becoming grist for the mill of Sartre's Marxism. Similarly, when Sartre notes that life would lose all meaning for him if he could no longer work (Beauvoir [1981] 1985: 104), one wonders if emphasizing one aspect of human being – the ability to reflect – negates other significant features of human life: so, relationship, friendship, love.

In some ways, Beauvoir's thought can be seen as a significant corrective to Sartre's at this point (Fullbrook and Fullbrook 1998: 2). Consciousness *'like it or not'* is embodied (Fullbrook and Fullbrook 1998: 60). Such a recognition necessitates a more detailed discussion of the complex relationship between human being as both transcendent and immanent. I am both consciousness that transcends my physical placing in the world, and I am immanent, in the sense that I am a physical being. Beauvoir claims that, to avoid bad faith, the existentialist description of an inauthentic existence, one must embody both of these features in one's life (Fullbrook and Fullbrook 1998: 66, 88). I like this: it resonates with the Aristotelian claim that human happiness is to be found through living a balanced life. In this case, rather than emphasize transcendent possibilities above physical existence, or physical existence above transcendence, one must integrate both features into the meaningful human life. In practice, Beauvoir does not seem able to maintain this balanced position, emphasizing transcendence in much the same way as Sartre. As Pilardi puts it, for Beauvoir 'subjectivity is not immanence; it is transcendence, an engagement in the world' (Pilardi 1999: 13). How Beauvoir understands these terms will become clearer when we turn our attention to her discussion of the female later in this chapter.

Undoubtedly, the notion of transcendence is given a this-worldly twist in existentialist thinking, and it is this element that I shall build upon. At the same time, recognizing the significance of embodiment means that the fear of death and the desire to transcend it will live on in its message. This is particularly noticeable in the work of Sartre. Whereas Heidegger views death as a positive boundary which demarcates the limits and scope of human life, for Sartre, death reveals the absurdity of the human condition: 'it is absurd that we are born; it is absurd that we die' (Sartre [1943] 1969: 547). And this is an important insight. Accepting embodiment does not necessarily lead to an optimistic account of human being. Indeed, there may be something peculiarly tragic about human life, given that we have the ability to transcend the physical through thought, but at the same time, like all animals, we are destined to die.

In Beauvoir's thought, this sense that human life is fundamentally tragic takes on a more explicitly gendered shape: if *women* are to escape the absurdity of the human condition, they must escape the immanence of biological experience that subsumes them in the physical world of decay and death. In this way, woman's biological function connects her intimately with death, and freedom for the female, while involving a change in societal mores, also lies in overcoming the bodily processes that invariably define her. In the existentialist schema of Sartre and Beauvoir, the body and biological life are ultimately devalued and desanctified in precisely the same way as in the Christian theology that they are at pains to reject.

Sartre: human mortality

Death is given a pivotal role in Sartre's system. It is a constant present, a possibility that renders all the tasks and hopes of life absurd. All human decisions are made against this backdrop (Sartre [1943] 1969: 171); all decisions are faintly pathetic because of the knowledge that death may cut short all one's aspirations and projects ([1943] 1969: 547). If a driving force of Sartre's philosophy is to return the individual to the centre of human life and action, it is death which stands as the potential (and indeed actual) obliterator of that same individual: 'By death, the for-itself is changed forever into an in-itself in that it has slipped entirely into the past'([1943] 1969: 115).[2]

The horror of this transformation does not cease with the death of the subject. If anything, what happens to the subject after death is perceived as the ultimate horror, for death delivers the 'I' into the hands of the 'Other', that metaphysical opponent who in Sartrean thought is always seeking to turn the sovereign subject into an object. For Sartre, the crucial difference between life and death lies in this, for, in death, I am suddenly placed in the hands of the Other. The way my life is seen after my death is no longer in my hands, but in the hands of countless 'Others' who surround me ([1943] 1969: 541). One only has to consider the way in which the contemporary media deals with the lives of people killed in tragic circumstances to get something of the horror that Sartre feels. When Diana, Princess of Wales, was killed in a car crash, she ceased to be a real individual and was portrayed alternately as a saint, a Sloane, a slut, or whatever other qualities the commentator deemed fit to project on to her. In a thought system that seeks to prioritize the autonomous creation of one's own life, it is easy to understand why Sartre would view such post-mortem manipulation with dread. My life is no longer in my own hands, but in the hands of the Other.

Not surprisingly, if death is painted in such terms, the desire to evade it becomes strong. For Sartre, such evasion will not take the form of some post-mortem existence, for what concerns him is locating human existence in this world, not in some hypothetical other world. Indeed, he is at pains to accept that death is a 'natural' phenomenon which signifies 'the return to nature' and which asserts that the individual is ultimately 'a part of nature' (Beauvoir [1981] 1985: 432). By way of contrast, Sartre's method relies on highlighting the potential transcendence open to the individual, and in so doing suggests a way of erecting a buffer against the cold reality of inevitable death. Perhaps almost inevitably this leads to the conclusion that it is through his writing that he will achieve a kind of immortality (Beauvoir [1981] 1985: 413). It is the ability to transcend the mundane reality of physical life through intellectual – be that academic or political – pursuits that appears to characterize human being for Sartre. Indeed, it is with the advent of humanity that meaning is introduced to the world, and Sartre shows his debt to Kant here. With human life comes rationality and the ability to give meaning to this world, to stand out from this world. Thus 'man' for Sartre *is* transcendence: 'Man, being transcendence, establishes the meaningful by his very coming into the world' (Sartre [1943] 1969: 602).

There is something powerful and positive about this idea. The human enterprise is to create meaning, to explore with wonder the world in which we find ourselves. It is tempting to read such ennobling statements as incorporating human being as a whole; in other words, women are included within the male generic that Sartre uses when describing this possibility. Yet such a conclusion will not stand when one turns one's attention to the role of the feminine/female in Sartre's thought; his reflections suggest something of the problematic nature of the physical world for the Sartrean individual. He argues that transcendence can be achieved only if what he characterizes as 'the feminine' is overcome. The feminine stands for the world against which the individual must 'stand out'/exist. Of course, it could be argued that the feminine and the female need not be equated. At this point, consideration must be given to Sartre's understanding of woman, for, while he apparently does not discuss her in *Being and Nothingness*, his rejection of the feminine can be linked to a negative account of woman in his thought and experience.

During the series of interviews that she conducted with Sartre between August and September 1974 (cf. Beauvoir [1981] 1985: 131–445), Beauvoir raises the question of Sartre's relationships with women. Before turning to the metaphysical construction of the feminine in *Being and Nothingness*, it is worth considering Sartre's account of his relations with women and his attitude towards them, for this suggests that, far from the feminine standing as a category distinct from biological and social femaleness, the one is irrevocably linked with the other.

Sartre reflects upon the affairs he had outside of the primary relationship with Beauvoir, which does appear to have been a mature relationship where intellectual exchange was as important as emotional and sexual love. Yet his affairs suggest a more polarized understanding of the roles of male and female. Sartre notes that the playing of parts was vital to these relationships: his was to be 'the active and reasonable one; the woman's role was on the emotional plane' (Beauvoir

[1981] 1985: 298). Similarly, during sexual intercourse, his was always the active role: as Beauvoir interjects, 'you were never aware of yourself as a passive object' ([1981] 1985: 314).

Now, such reflections are highly significant for Sartre's metaphysics. In attributing emotion to women, the stage is set for an account of the feminine that distances women from reason. In his thought, emotion signifies consciousness 'asleep' (Sartre [1971] 1999: 78); or, as Warnock puts it, emotion for Sartre signifies 'sinking into an inferior mode of consciousness' ([1971] 1999: 12). We should bear this in mind when we consider the way transcendence is to be achieved under Sartre's schema. Already, there is the sense that it will be difficult to maintain a distinction between feminine and female.

This becomes apparent when Sartre's experience of the otherness of women is considered. The other, as we have noted, is a key category in Sartrean thought. During these interviews, Sartre suggests a felt apprehension of woman as other. His childhood fantasies of defending a European girl from a 'Chinaman' suggests not only woman as filling the role of other, but also any non-European (Beauvoir [1981] 1985: 227). Moreover, 'the Look' which fixes the subject as object is attributed to women when Sartre discusses the comments that first made him aware of his own ugliness ([1981] 1985: 309–10).

Let us now consider how such experiences inform his metaphysics. An important starting place is found in Sartre's account of the body. While his existentialism is at pains to reject the soul/body dualism of the Western tradition, in practice he maintains the inferiority of the body. While he accepts that 'the body is a necessary characteristic of the for-itself' (Sartre [1943] 1969: 309), there is a sense of alienation from the physical self in his writings. For example, 'the body-for-itself is never a given which I can know. It is there everywhere as the surpassed; it exists only in so far as I escape it by nihilating myself' (1969: 309). This account has ramifications for the way in which femaleness is understood. We have noted the way in which Sartre identifies the women with whom he had affairs with physicality. By opposing the immanence of the body to the transcendence of the 'I', Sartre reveals something of the problematic formulation of femaleness: 'the body manifests my contingency' ([1943] 1969: 310), and therefore if the 'I' is to attain the transcendence which comes through freedom, the body/female must be overcome.

Yet there is undoubtedly a tension in Sartre's account of the body. While viewing it as problematic, as that which is subsumed in the matter of the world, he recognizes it 'as the necessary condition of the existence of the world and as the contingent realization of this condition' ([1943] 1969: 328). This is vital to an existentialist account of the self. I am placed in the world at a particular point in history. My race, class, nationality, physiology and character are all referred to by Sartre as vital when understanding my response to the world. Interestingly, he ignores the role which sex/sexuality contributes to the placement of the self. This suggests either a conscious evasion of the gendered nature of his account of the other, or an inability to recognize, as Beauvoir will, the fundamental significance of gender. Yet if the placing of the body is of fundamental importance when determining how one lives in the world, there is also a sense that the body can be controlled, despite the rejection of dualism. As Sartre puts it, 'I cannot be crippled without choosing to be crippled' ([1943] 1969: 328). In other words, it is how I respond to my physical placing that matters. As Beauvoir shows, it is more difficult than this, for socialization cannot be dismissed so lightly.

The tension in Sartre's writing, between rejecting dualism and re-creating it, may go some way to explaining his implicit understanding of woman. Of crucial importance to his account of the self is the oppositional/conflictual placing of 'the Other'. The Other is defined as 'the indispensable mediator between myself and me'. In seeking to know myself, I must recognize that 'I *am* as the Other sees me' ([1943] 1969: 222). It is the power of the Other's 'look' (see Sartre [1943] 1969: pt 3, ch. 1, section IV) that gives rise to the conflictual nature of this relationship. In the Other's look, I become an object in the world, defined by others:

> To apprehend myself as seen is, in fact, to apprehend myself as seen *in the world* and from the standpoint of the world. The look does not carve me out in the universe. ([1943] 1969: 263)

If I am to remain a subject, I must render the Other into an object which can be controlled. It is here that the identification of woman with the Other starts to form. We have already considered Sartre's personal experience of woman as possessor of the look that defines him as 'ugly'. Now, Sartre focuses on the desire to assimilate the Other ([1943] 1969: 365), and thus to control the way in which the Other sees me. Under such an account, sexual relations are defined as the original attempt to hold the Other's free subjectivity ([1943] 1969:

382). Possession of the Other comes to define the goal of sexual love.[3] In offering such an account of sexual relations, Sartre reveals the male-centredness of his approach. At one point he writes: 'we desire *a particular woman*' ([1943] 1969: 384; my emphasis). While this may simply reflect his experience as a male heterosexual, when placed in the context of his sexual experiences it takes on a normative role. In another place, the identification of woman with the world is made more obvious when Sartre positions her amid all the other objects that the subject seeks to possess:

> Each possessed object which raises itself on the foundation of the world, manifests the entire world, just as a beloved woman manifests the sky, the shore, the sea which surround her when she appeared. ([1943] 1969: 596)

Woman, so far, appears as Other, linked with the world and the immanence of being. Sartre makes a further connection, suggesting that woman and sexuality are peculiarly linked. These ideas are grounded in Hegel's claim that 'the difference between man and woman is the difference between animal and plant' (cited in B. Clack 1999: 177). Such a claim informs Sartre's contention that 'if sex were to appear as an organ, it could be only one manifestation of the vegetative life' ([1943] 1969: 397). Such an idea will be shown to inform his characterization of woman, ultimately leading to the identification between sex, death and the female.

At one point in *Being and Nothingness*, Sartre, as part of his attempt to offer a 'psychoanalysis of *things*' ([1943] 1969: 600) analyses the qualities of slime and sliminess.[4] Early on he suggests a vague connection with women, writing of the quality of the 'sticky' as being akin to 'the flattening out of the full breasts of a woman who is lying on her back' ([1943] 1969: 608). If one pauses to reflect on this definition it appears rather odd. Visualize such an image and the word 'sticky' does not spring automatically to mind. It is only when the connection between the female and contingency is made that a clearer sense emerges of what Sartre has in mind when he uses this image. The female is 'a sweet, clinging, dependent threat to male freedom' (Collins and Pierce 1980: 117). She represents the world that seeks to subsume the subject individual in immanence. Elsewhere, Sartre recollects visiting a psychologist who showed him various pictures and invited him to pick out one which best represented speed. He chose a boat 'because it was

breaking free of the water'. He goes on to say that 'the water represented contingency. The boat was hard, well built, solid' (Beauvoir
[1981] 1985: 316). The oceanic abyss of the chaotic female is what
must be avoided.

The depiction of stickiness in *Being and Nothingness* develops into
a discussion of the peculiarly *feminine* quality of slime: it yields, it
offers 'a moist and feminine sucking', a quality with echoes of the
abyss and death, as 'it draws me to it as the bottom of a precipice
might draw me' (Sartre [1943] 1969: 609). The connection between
women/the feminine and death is thus quickly established. Writing of
the quality of slime, it appears that Sartre is alluding to the reality of
the end to which we must all come. In language that resonates with
descriptions of decomposition, Sartre sees slime as 'the revenge of the
In-itself'; it is 'a sickly-sweet, feminine revenge' ([1943] 1969: 609).
Such language connects with Augustine's depiction of the sexual as
that which pulls one into the abyss of natural life. Sartre's humanism
betrays a similar suspicion of sexual intimacy.

Characterizing slime in such a way suggests that there is a deeper
connection being made here. Slime is not simply a reality which alludes to decomposition; it also resonates with the condition by which
we enter the world in the first place: the sweat, blood and mucus of
birth. Birth and death are located in the feminine. In Sartre's novel
Nausea, it is not the fear of death that causes the protagonist Roquentin
such *Angst*: it is the sheer gratuitousness of being which he finds sick-
ening. There is, he realizes, no reason for existence: we are simply
thrown into the world (Sartre [1938] 1965: 188). But this sense of
existence as threat is not gender-neutral. The female body is linked
with the appalling fecundity of nature:

> I toyed absent-mindedly with her sex under the bedclothes . . . I let my
> arm move along the woman's side and suddenly I saw a little garden
> with low, wide-spreading trees from which huge hairy leaves were hang-
> ing. Ants were running everywhere, centipedes and moths. There were
> some even more horrible animals: their bodies were made of slices of
> toast such as you put under roast pigeon; they were walking sideways
> with crab-like legs . . . Behind the cacti and the Barbary fig trees, the
> Velleda of the municipal park was pointing to her sex. 'This park smells
> of vomit,' I shouted. ([1938] 1965: 88–9)

This Bosch-like image is fascinating, for it is not death at this point
that horrifies Roquentin: it is the multiplicity of life-forms which popu-

late the world. Fertility is viewed with horror, and, as the dream becomes more disturbing, the image of the woman pointing to her womb suggests that the horror of the female responsible for such life underpins it all. The fecundity described in this passage cannot, however, be separated from death. The life that the female creates is destined for death, and the horror of the female organs as death-dealing as well as life-giving permeates the other memorable description of a woman in this novel:

> The cashier is at her counter. I know her well: she is red-haired like myself; she has some sort of stomach disease. She is rotting quietly under her skirts with a melancholy smile, like the smell of violets which is sometimes given off by decomposing bodies. I shudder from head to foot. It is . . . it is she who is waiting for me. (Sartre [1938] 1965: 84)

We come from slime and we go to slime, and ultimately, despite the existentialist project of transcendence, no one can avoid such a destiny. In both birth and death the individual is ill-defined, dependent, dissolved, destroyed, and these are concepts which challenge the humanistic transcendental ethic offered by the existentialist:

> The slimy offers a horrible image; it is horrible in itself for a consciousness to *become slimy*. This is because the being of the slimy is a soft clinging, there is a sly solidarity and complicity of all its leech like parts, a vague, soft effort made by each to individualize itself, followed by a falling back and flattening out that is emptied of the individual, sucked in on all sides by the substance. (Sartre [1943] 1969: 610)

Despite the existentialist project of transcendence, no one can avoid returning to slime after death. Now, Sartre denies that his description of slime is a description of the fear of death, or of nothingness, but maintains that it is connected to the horrors of non-consciousness or non-subjective being ([1943] 1969: 611). His disgust with, and inability to eat, 'crustaceans, oysters, shellfish' suggests a horror not only of mucus but of prying a creature from a snug home, thus creating 'a gaping hole in its substance' (Beauvoir [1981] 1985: 333). Yet the unwillingness to connect such repulsion with death seems disingenuous, to say the least. While he rejects the idea of birth trauma as leading to the preoccupation with 'the gluey, the sticky, the hazy . . . holes in the sand and in the earth, caves' (Sartre [1943] 1969: 612), which seems to arise from the child's pre-psychic experience, his own account of female sexuality links it conclusively with the sliminess and void of non-being. Woman is described 'in the form of a hole' ([1943] 1969: 614); 'the obscenity of the feminine sex is that of everything which "gapes open"' ([1943] 1969: 613). The horror of the slime which engulfs is paralleled with the female sex organs:

> Her sex is a mouth and a voracious mouth which devours the penis – a fact which can easily lead to the idea of castration. The amorous act is the castration of the man; but this is above all because sex is a hole. ([1943] 1969: 614)

The connection between women, sexuality and death is thus complete. As she is peculiarly responsible for birth, so woman becomes responsible for death, and thus, in Sartre's transcendental ethic, woman is to be evaded just as an immortal ethic will distance itself from the body. The obsession with finding a life outside this physical world continues even in as self-consciously humanist an ethic as Sartre's existentialism, and it is worth noting with Beauvoir that 'the values of Nature, [and] Fecundity' (Beauvoir [1981] 1985: 316) are of little interest to him.

Simone de Beauvoir: the rejection of sexuality

The connections between Sartre's work and that of Simone de Beauvoir have been explored in some depth (cf. Fullbrook and Fullbrook 1993; 1998; Simons 1986). Like Sartre, Beauvoir accepts the existentialist view of the creation of the self. In similar vein, she views the human ability to transcend/stand out from the physical world as the distinguishing mark of the human. Where she differs from Sartre is in developing an existentialist ethic that considers specifically female existence and experience. However, like Sartre she implicitly accepts the symbolic links made between the female body and death. For her, freedom becomes the ability to transcend one's physical placing, and this has a particular impact on how she views female liberation. It is female bodily experience that is problematic for Beauvoir, and it is the perceived limitations of the female body that must be overcome if woman is to be truly free.

As we have seen, in Sartre's work an implicit connection is made between woman and 'the other'. While in Sartre's schema the other need not be female, there is a sense in which s/he is assumed to be so. So, sexual intercourse becomes a battle between the subject and the object for supremacy, a conflictual understanding that is not without its critics (cf. Dilman 1987: 72). Beauvoir picks up on this assumption and makes it explicit. Historically, she points out, man has always defined woman as 'the Other' (Beauvoir [1949] 1972: 16). Indeed, woman plays a crucial role in defining male identity. Writing in terms which in more recent years have been adopted by Luce Irigaray, Beauvoir notes that woman 'is the mirror in which the male, Narcissus-like, contemplates himself' ([1949] 1972: 217). Woman has no role but this in patriarchal society: she simply provides man with the image he wishes to project of himself. In this way, Beauvoir adopts and yet challenges Sartre's account of 'the Look'. For Sartre, the gaze of the Other had the potential to render the subject an object. Beauvoir suggests that this is not strictly the case: the male subject *needs* the look of the female object to reflect him as he wishes to be seen. Woman thus becomes the projection of male desires, fears, loves and hates ([1949] 1972: 229). As such, it should not surprise us that the female will come to represent both sexuality and death, and that in her these two aspects of human existence will become one.[5]

Beauvoir's project is not simply to provide evidence of the historical oppression of women (although she does this most effectively); she is also concerned to offer a potential way out of the mirror for womankind. The more woman asserts her own self, the more female otherness will cease to exist ([1949] 1972: 174). Yet how she is to do this is extremely problematic: as Irigaray has pointed out, woman's role in patriarchal society has left her devoid of a history, a language, and a community from which to achieve this new world (cf. Irigaray 1985b). Perhaps it is not surprising, then, that Beauvoir's solution should ultimately accept masculinist accounts of what is valuable in human life. As Jean Grimshaw puts it, Beauvoir tends to regard 'the qualities and capacities which she sees as masculine as those which women should emulate or strive to achieve' (Grimshaw 1986: 46). This becomes particularly clear when Beauvoir addresses the question of the female body. Implicit in her account is an assumption that the mind or mental life is superior to the body. Thus she, like Sartre, ultimately puts forward an account of human life that is not so very different from the dualist self which they apparently seek to reject, but which, given the acceptance of Cartesianism, is perhaps difficult to avoid.

While at pains to argue that the dualist rejection of the body as crucial to the formation of the self is misguided, there is a tension in this account that becomes apparent with Beauvoir's specific analysis of the female body. The body is peculiarly problematic for woman, as it is her body which has rendered woman 'the victim of the species' (Beauvoir [1949] 1972: 52). She has been defined as 'a womb, an ovary' ([1949] 1972: 35), and is thus imprisoned in her sex in a way in which the man's role in reproduction will not ensnare the male. (The defining of woman according to her biological function may go some way to explaining why Beauvoir's solution will be to reject the female 'role'.) Indeed, the extent to which she is caught by the reproductive process is evident not only when she is 'creating' a new life (although as we shall see, Beauvoir disputes the authenticity of applying the word 'creation' to the 'natural' process of reproduction). Menstruation is similarly problematic, for it suggests that her body is 'an obscure, alien thing. . .Woman, like man, *is* her body; but her body is something other than herself' ([1949] 1972: 61). It has its own mysterious operations that continually convince woman that she is not in control of her destiny.

This theme is continued when Beauvoir describes the qualities of male and female bodies. The male sex organ is 'simple and neat as a finger' ([1949] 1972: 406), while 'the feminine sex organ is mysterious even to the woman herself, concealed, mucous, and humid, as it is; it bleeds each month, it is often sullied with body fluids, it has a secret and perilous life of its own' ([1949] 1972: 406). Nothing positive can be derived from such an organ, and one wonders what Beauvoir would make of works that seek to establish the power, indeed wisdom, of the menstrual bleed (cf. Shuttle and Redgrove 1986). The act of sex is also viewed as different for men and women, suggesting that the biological reality of being female differs fundamentally from being male: 'Man dives upon his prey like the eagle and the hawk; woman lies in wait like the carnivorous plant, the bog, in which insects and children are swallowed up' ([1949] 1972: 407).

Beauvoir even describes feminine sexual desire as 'the soft throbbing of a mollusc' ([1949] 1972: 407). Such language not only suggests a rather negative view of female embodiment; it also resonates with the Sartrean descriptions of slime considered in the previous section. Of course, it could be that Beauvoir is using such language to highlight the way in which female sexual experience has been dismissed in the Western tradition. What seems more likely is that she has grasped the significance of embodiment, but is aware of its tragic potential.

My body can be an ill body, a body which threatens consciousness. This would seem to be true for men *and* women. The difficulty lies in the way in which Beauvoir seems to problematize only the female body. Her dismissive attitude to the female role in reproduction is perhaps a case in point.

According to Beauvoir, birth is not a truly creative act: 'she does not really make the body [of the child], it makes itself within her' ([1949] 1972: 513). Ever the existentialist, she argues that truly creative acts originate in liberty, and therefore the child is 'only a gratuitous cellular growth, a brute fact of nature as contingent on circumstances as death' ([1949] 1972: 514). In making such comments Beauvoir implicitly accepts patriarchal accounts of what constitutes true creativity. Strangely, her comments appear to reiterate Plato's distinction between physical procreation and spiritual creativity. Moreover, it is 'not in giving life but in risking life that man is raised above the animal; that is why superiority has been accorded in humanity not to the sex that brings forth but to that which kills' ([1949] 1972: 95–6). Now, there may be a sense in which Beauvoir is stating such claims with a view to critiquing them. However, nowhere does she give a positive role to the female as giver of life – hardly surprising, as the existentialist project is to stand out from the world, not to be caught in its natural processes and cycles. Despite claims to the contrary, the privileging of transcendence over immanence is implicitly accepted by Beauvoir (cf. Fullbrook and Fullbrook 1998). Both of these qualities may be grounded in human experience of the world: but the female has come to be connected with immanence, the male with transcendence. While Beauvoir is critical of the way the gendered account of these concepts has arisen, discounting such claims as 'vagaries of the mind' ([1949] 1972: 44), she unconsciously privileges transcendence over immanence. Thus she writes with what seems a sense of horror that 'the feminine belly is the symbol of immanence, of depth' ([1949] 1972: 208). By way of contrast, the existentialist project is viewed thus:

> Every subject . . . achieves liberty only through a continual *reaching out* towards other liberties. ([1949] 1972: 28; my emphasis)

Similarly, for the subject to justify 'his' existence 'involves an undefined need to transcend himself [*sic*], to engage in freely chosen projects' ([1949] 1972: 29). It is at this point that liberation is a possibility for the female. Woman does not have to be subsumed in the processes of the body; she does have a choice. She, too, can become a transcendent ([1949] 1972: 82). The possibility of achieving transcendence becomes for Beauvoir the feminist project, the hope that 'transcendence may prevail over immanence' ([1949] 1972: 164). The acceptance of a masculinist distancing from the world seems, then, to categorize Beauvoir's thought. Her feminism merely asks that women be admitted to this process of distancing the self from the physical world. It is not surprising, then, that she should view the suppression of matriarchy and the female as 'a necessary stage in the history of humanity' ([1949] 1972: 106–7).

In privileging transcendence over immanence, Beauvoir develops a further theme that is present in Sartre's thought. Sartre makes a connection – at times implicit – between women, sex and death. Beauvoir's critical comments of the female body lead her ultimately to make the same connection. Of course, it is difficult to say how much she agreed with this connection: after all, she makes her comments in the midst of her analysis of the socialization and interpretation of woman, and a crucial part of her project is to present women with the possibility of a transcendental option. But, even if she makes such comments in order to reject them, they have a peculiar resonance with her own comments about motherhood and the female body. For a start, her claim that the female body has been linked purely with immanence leads her to suggest that 'man' identifies woman with nature and thus with death:

> He exploits her [Nature], but she crushes him, he is born of her and dies in her; she is the source of his being and the realm that he subjugates to his will . . . Now ally, now enemy, she appears as the dark chaos from whence life wells up, as this life itself, and as the over-yonder towards which life tends. ([1949] 1972: 175–6)

Present within this analysis is an awareness of the ambivalence of the mother figure. She gives life, but in doing so condemns 'man' to mortality and thus to inevitable death. In developing this point, Beauvoir builds upon Sartre's own analysis of slime, while making far more explicit than he does himself the connection between sex and death:

> This quivering jelly which is elaborated in the womb (the womb, secret and sealed like a tomb) evokes too clearly the soft viscosity of carrion for him not to turn shuddering away. Wherever life is in the making – germination, fermentation – it arouses disgust because it is made only

in being destroyed; the slimy embryo begins the cycle that is completed in the putrefaction of death. Because he is horrified by needlessness and death, man feels horror at having been engendered; he would fain deny his animal ties; through the fact of his birth murderous Nature has a hold upon him. ([1949] 1972: 178)

If we had any doubt that slime is linked with decomposition, Beauvoir takes the relevant step in her analysis. Moreover, Beauvoir has made a powerful connection between the fear of death and the fear of woman. Indeed, she makes this claim explicit when she writes that the male horror of woman is precisely 'the horror of his own carnal contingence, which he projects on her' ([1949] 1972: 180). Male sexual experience if anything makes this connection stronger; ejaculation – 'the little death' – is indeed 'a promise of death' ([1949] 1972: 194). Yet in making this connection Beauvoir sees in male sexuality the struggle between transcendence and immanence:

> Man glories in the phallus when he thinks of it as transcendence and activity . . . but he is ashamed of it when he sees it as merely passive flesh through which he is the plaything of the dark forces of life. ([1949] 1972: 195)

This is a highly promising critique of the way in which the fear of death underpins hopes of immortality/transcendence, and which, in turn, leads to a negative account of sexuality. Yet while writing so powerfully of the desires that drive the need for a symbol that transfigures the vulnerability of the penis into the power of the phallus, Beauvoir herself cannot escape falling similarly in thrall to the desire for transcendence. While these passages suggest a recognition of the way in which male sexuality has shaped our thought forms, she maintains a sense of the negativity of the flesh which necessitates the privileging of the possibility of an existence that transcends ordinary, mutable human being – albeit an existence to be found in the here and now, rather than in some hypothetical other-world. She may capture exactly the sense that the fear of woman is wrapped up with the fear of death; yet she cannot escape accepting this self-same conclusion:

> Woman's fate is bound up with that of perishable things; in losing them they lose all. Only a free subject, asserting himself as above and beyond duration of things, can check all decay. ([1949] 1972: 613)

Freedom can thus be equated with transcendence, and the balance between transcendence and immanence, promised by her reflections on embodiment, is not maintained. Only when woman attains the same attitude to life and the same commitment to transcendent activity as the male, can she really be free ([1949] 1972: 689). Of course, the hope offered by such a life is vainglorious, for Beauvoir has to accept the reality of biological death that will kill the consciousness of the subject. Even a being who attains this transcendent dimension will die.

All of which renders Beauvoir's existentialist ethic for women's liberation rather problematic. The natural world remains something to be overcome, and there is a real desire on her part to relieve woman of the burden of biology. Now, when we see this alongside her knowledge of the history of women's oppression, we can understand the logic of her approach: the essentialist account of woman which focuses on her role in prolonging the species has to be overcome if woman is to be able to function as a whole individual in the world. When a philosopher such as Otto Weininger, writing at the beginning of the twentieth century, suggests that woman cannot be an individual because she is so subsumed in the things of the natural world, his is not the voice of an isolated maverick. Rather he is simply reiterating the kind of comments to be found in the philosophies of figures as diverse as Plato, Aristotle, Kant and Hegel.[6]

Beauvoir's solution to this state of affairs is simple: rather than seek an alternative engagement with the facts presented by the physical world, she suggests ways in which women might resist such stereotyping. Most notably, motherhood is to be rejected. But such responses are based upon the idea that other ways of being a mother are not possible, and Beauvoir does not adequately think through alternative ways of child-rearing and parenting. Given contemporary discussions of the roles open to men and women as parents, Beauvoir's discussion seems, at least on this point, a little dated.

It is, then, only through adopting a form of transcendence over her environment that woman will really be free. In accepting this conclusion, Beauvoir fails to recognize the way in which patriarchy has been built upon precisely this distinction between the physical, immanent world and the possibility of an existence that evades the fact that we are animals – albeit highly developed animals (Ryle [1949] 1963: 310) – who, like all animals, must die. Rather than balancing these two aspects of human life, Beauvoir, like Sartre, ends by subjugating the immanent to the transcendent.

Conclusion: balancing transcendence and immanence

Consideration of the existentialist ideas of both Sartre and Beauvoir suggests something of the continuing power of the paradigm of transcendence for understanding human being. It would seem that it is extremely difficult to escape from the desire for some feature of human being which might provide an escape from the mutability and vulnerability of existence. Despite the promise that Sartrean existentialism will hold together the immanent and transcendent, the physical and the mental, in practice, it is the possibility of a position that transcends biological existence that dominates their thinking.

Roger Scruton makes an important point when criticizing Beauvoir's position. He notes that Beauvoir's Kantian feminism 'is at war with the truth that we are our bodies, and, in separating personal freedom entirely from biological destiny, it is misled by a transcendental illusion' (Scruton [1986] 1994: 260). This highlights almost exactly the way in which existentialist thinking coheres with the kind of essentialist answers offered by Plato and Augustine: in seeking an answer to the problems raised by mortality, the body is ignored in favour of the mind. Yet it should also be noted that Beauvoir, in particular, identifies the problems that arise from physical existence: it is not always a positive thing to recognize that we are, fundamentally, animals.[7] With embodiment comes the possibility of suffering through illness or assault, and the recognition that death stands at the end of existence. A more appropriate response may be to recognize that there are no easy answers to the problems death raises. It may be that we have to accept the fundamentally tragic nature of human life and the limited possibility of an effective response. All we can do is continue the human enterprise to create meaning, finding in love, friendship and relationship, political action, art and music, ways of making the most of the time that we have as conscious beings.

Such reflections may suggest a possible way forward which does not oppose transcendence to immanence, but grounds the one within the other. Like that of Sartre and Beauvoir, Sigmund Freud's work is grounded in a thorough-going materialism which understands human being as part of the natural world. Like them, he makes a connection between sex and death. However, this connection is made rather differently, and, in doing so, Freud suggests an understanding of human life which makes possible a spirituality grounded not in the transcendence of the physical, but in the transience of human existence. It is to his account that we must now turn.

3

Eros, Thanatos and the Human Self: Sigmund Freud

Introduction

It is no exaggeration to claim that Freud's account of the human individual, and the general psychoanalytic approach that stems from it, was the most influential way of considering the nature of the human person in the twentieth century. Freud's influence is felt in the 'psychobabble' of American popular culture, in the films of Woody Allen, in the growing recognition that it is better to confront the 'issues' of one's life than to be silent. The terms he uses have become common currency: 'repression', 'ego', 'id', 'libido' are terms which find their contemporary meanings – albeit somewhat inaccurately – in his work. Theoretically, his ideas form the basis for the work of Jacques Lacan, darling of the post-modern *literati*, of some feminists, and even of those practitioners of 'radical orthodoxy' who wish to use such views to remake Christianity.[1] For a study such as this, which seeks to formulate a spirituality not upon the evasion of sex and death, but on an acceptance of these basic features of human life, Freud's ideas are equally significant.

So far, we have considered the different ways in which the notion of transcendence has influenced constructions of spirituality and human being in the Western tradition: we saw how it drives the different ideas put forward by Plato and Augustine, Sartre and Beauvoir. Human being was ultimately understood through those features that distance us from our ordinary physical placing in and experience of the world. Consideration of Freud's opinions brings to the fore the immanent features associated with being human. Freud focuses on what human physicality tells us about human being. It is through an engagement with his account of the self that we might move some way towards an understanding of human being that seeks to unite the transcendent and immanent aspects of our humanity.

Freud's work suggests that conflict is the defining feature of the human self. This is expressed in two ways. Primarily, there is the struggle to repress the knowledge of our 'true' bodily nature: while we might like to think of ourselves as 'like gods', we are gods with genitals and anuses (Becker 1973: 51). We reproduce like animals, and the need to defecate expresses the fact that we are corporeal beings who must eat to live, and that eventually we will cease to do so. Human culture, as we shall see, is thus defined by the attempt to overcome the knowledge of human mortality. Similarly, the Western construction of human spirituality has involved the attempt to transcend these fundamental facts of human existence.

At the same time, Freud is concerned with the idea of a basic struggle between two instincts. It is significant that it should be 'two', for, despite Freud's rejection of the dualist self, his own work is frequently expressed in terms of the conflicts that arise between dualities. In his early publications, this conflict is located in the ego, and concerns the struggle between the pleasure principle and the reality principle. In his later work, this conflict is between two instincts, ultimately expressed as eros, or the sex instinct, and thanatos, or the death instinct.

This chapter will explore both of these conflicts. Freud's work may appear antagonistic to the spiritual life, and there is indeed a strongly anti-religious trend in his thought. I intend to suggest that a this-worldly spirituality can be advanced which grounds itself in the kind of reflection upon – not rejection of – human sexuality and mortality that so exercised Freud. A form of transcendence develops in Freud's work that is grounded, not in the kind of distance from physical human life which ultimately colours the account of human being offered by Sartre and Beauvoir, but in the things of this world, valued and appreciated in themselves. In his ideas we get an intimation – albeit rather muted – of what a meaningful account of human life might be liked, based upon a unified account of the transcendent and immanent features of human being.

The role of the instincts

The major innovation in Freud's account of the self lies in the leading role that he gives to the instinctual life. If previous Western accounts of the self focus on those features of human experience that distinguish us from the rest of the animal world – most notably the ability to reason and the phenomenon of consciousness[2] – Freud's account concentrates on those aspects of our humanity which link us most closely with animality. He may write of the 'ego' ('das Ich'), but invariably this is viewed as a fragile construction in thrall to the powers of the unconscious. He is at pains to resist those accounts of the self which emphasize ratiocination, for, while they may may tell us much about this 'sick animal' man, they invariably ignore those features which are not accessible to reason – namely, the instincts and the unconscious, the 'id' ('das Es'), to use Freud's terminology.[3] The emphasis that Freud places on the unconscious and the instinctual may be innovative, but it is not without precedent. In Nietzsche's work there is a similar recognition of the power of the instinctual. But it is with Freud that this account of human being attains its fullest expression. It should be noted at this point that Freud's ideas are constantly open to change and development, and this is reflected in the different stages of his writing. As we shall see, this is of crucial importance for understanding his account of the relationship between sex and death, suggesting a more complex theory of human selfhood than that with which he is sometimes credited.

Freud makes that which is not obvious of key importance to the definition of the human self. Such a move makes sense only if it is understood in relation to the key role of repression in his thought. Civilization, as he puts it in an early work, is 'built upon the suppression of instincts' (Freud [1908] 1985: 38). In a slightly later paper he defines what he means by 'an instinct'. It is not a force with a momentary impact; rather its influence is constant. It cannot be fled from, for it comes from within, not from without. It is 'a concept on the frontier between the mental and the somatic' (Freud [1915b] 1984: 118), and thus is located upon the battleground where the need for socialization – obtained by repression – comes into conflict with the animalistic features of humanity. In 'Beyond the Pleasure Principle' (1920), this definition is further qualified: an instinct is now defined as 'an urge inherent in organic life to restore to an earlier state of things which the

living entity has been obliged to abandon under the pressure of external disturbing forces' (Freud [1920] 1984: 308–9). As we shall see,
this definition goes some way to explaining the shift away from simply considering one instinct – the sex instinct in relation to the pleasure principle – as the key focus for the cathexes of repression, towards
a more complex discussion of the conflict which arises between *two*
instincts: sex and death.[4]

Given his early definition of an instinct as that on the 'frontier between the mental and the somatic', it is perhaps not surprising that the
conflict Freud highlights in his early discussions of the instincts is between two mental functions: the 'pleasure principle' versus the 'reality
principle' (Freud [1911] 1984). At this stage in his writing it is the
conflict between elements within the developing ego that concerns him,
although the extent to which the subject is not conscious of this conflict suggests that already Freud's interest lies with the instinctual, and
thus with the unconscious. (It may also suggest something of the problematic nature of the Freudian unconscious highlighted by Sartre.)
Central to Freud's account of the self is the importance given to the
period of childhood, and particularly to the idea that the child is a
sexual being. As he puts it, 'the new-born baby brings sexuality with it
into the world' ([1907] 1977). In describing the significance of the sex
instinct for human development, Freud describes the child as 'poly-
morphously perverse' ([1905] 1977: 109), able to take pleasure from
every part of its body. This understanding is crucial to his account of
sexual development: the child moves from an oral stage, to an anal
stage, to a genital stage, finding pleasure in sucking, excreting/with-
holding excrement, and in masturbation.

At this stage in his theorizing, it is the development of the unconscious mental processes accompanying such behaviour that concerns
Freud. The primary mental process that he highlights is the 'pleasure
principle', the principle that seeks pleasure and avoids that which is
not pleasurable ([1911] 1984: 36). Its goals thus align it closely with
the sex instinct. But its desired outcome is not always achieved: disap-
pointment in attaining pleasure leads to the development of a new
principle of mental functioning, the 'reality principle': 'What was presented in the mind was no longer what was agreeable but what was
real, even if it happened to be disagreeable' ([1911] 1984: 37).

In this early work, Freud is rather vague as to what causes the construction of the reality principle, although this principle seems to have
much in common with the development of the 'superego' ('das Über-

Ich').[5] At this stage, he could be read as suggesting that this is a process which takes place with little direct influence from the child's parents or the world outside him.[6] The child becomes aware that reality will not always support his desire for pleasure, and thus introduces a 'reality principle' to his developing concepts. Freud's later thought suggests a more proactive role for the parents: conflict occurs when the child, previously shielded from reality by the parent, is taught that certain activities which give him pleasure are inappropriate, and that the only legitimate outlet for sexual experience lies with genital intercourse legalized by the state for the procreation of children.[7]

During this early stage in his thinking it is purely the sex instinct and its role in the development of the pleasure and reality principles which concerns Freud. It is the desire for pleasure that frames the child's world, and it is Freud's contention that the repression of such eclectic spheres for sexual expression leads to the often frustrated attempts of adults to find sexual fulfilment. In Freud's later thought this emphasis on conflict is developed rather differently. Instead of suggesting that there is one dominant instinct – the sex instinct and its mental development the pleasure principle – which comes into conflict with an external human authority, he argues for a more complex account of the instincts. With his later reflection comes the recognition of the powerful roles that both sex *and death* play in constructing the human self.

Eventually, Freud will argue that two main instincts govern human life: the life instinct ('eros') and the death instinct ('thanatos'). Initially, his move from a sole concern with the sex instinct into a dualistic account of the instincts isolates the sex instinct and the 'ego instincts' (Freud [1915b] 1984). The ego instincts consist of two features: those instincts that aim at self-preservation and those with a repressive function. We might want to question the idea of ascribing instinctual features to the ego at all: after all, it seems that for Freud the ego is itself a construction, rather than an innate given. This comment may explain his subsequent move to defining the two ruling instincts as those concerned with sex and death. In 'Beyond the pleasure principle', written five years after the discussion of the sex instinct and ego instincts in 'Instincts and their vicissitudes', he defines an instinct as the 'urge inherent in organic life to restore an earlier state of things which the living entity has been obliged to abandon under the pressure of external disturbing forces' (Freud [1920] 1984: 308–9). Such a definition suggests a connection between both sex and death: both can be equated to fundamental instincts, and both are concerned with the attempt to restore organic life to an earlier state of affairs.[8]

Of course, the dearth of evidence for such drives pushing towards a similar goal suggests a major problem for Freud's account. Freud's way out of this is to develop a mythical picture of a prehistoric past – a strategy which he also employs when considering the origins of religion (cf. Freud [1919] 1938), and which seems to suggest that scientific accounts of human being cannot stand alone. We need stories too. Indeed, if we accept that Freud is using such stories as creative engagements with the human condition, rather than as forms of pseudo-scientific explanation, a more creative engagement with his work might be possible. Freud himself suggests that the advocacy of such an approach may not be illegitimate. As he commences his speculative thoughts upon the origins of religion in *Totem and Taboo*, he makes the following comment: 'The reader need not fear that psychoanalysis, which first revealed the regular over-determination of psychic acts and formulations, will be tempted to derive anything so complicated as religion from a single source' ([1919] 1938: 138). Rather, Freud could be seen to be playing with ideas through using a literary form.[9] He is suggesting how things *might* have been, rather than saying that his stories provide definitive proof for the origin of religion.

A similar interpretation might be given to his imaginative accounts of the prehistoric past, although I accept that the overtly scientific language he uses might make it difficult to sustain the claim that he *thinks* he is writing literature rather than science! Prior to the development of higher forms of life, 'living substance was . . . constantly created afresh and easily dying' (Freud [1920] 1984: 311). As evolution progressed, so life made more 'complicated detours' ([1920] 1984: 311) before ending in death. The death instinct is thus related to these earliest forms of animate existence. Death is the 'final goal of all organic striving' ([1920] 1984: 210), when the animate being seeks a return to inanimate existence. Death is thus, perhaps surprisingly, viewed as an *internal* mechanism, and, while we may be more complex forms of life, we still have the desire to escape consciousness and return to inanimate matter. Freud's formulation of the 'nirvana principle' suggests a further connection between his biological and religious myth-making: religion under this account seems to be a feature of the death instinct (cf. Freud [1929] 1975). The desirability of death suggests something about the pessimistic way in which Freud views that which has habitually formed the focus for highly optimistic discussions of the human self: consciousness. For Freud, consciousness is problematic. It is the awareness that we have of ourselves which results in the futile attempts to escape our biological destiny. It is indeed consciousness that turns us into 'neurotic animals', struggling to repress the knowledge that, while we might be able to reflect upon our existence, ultimately we are destined for death and decay.[10]

While the attempt to make a return to earlier forms of existence dominates both instincts (and renders both in some ways conservative (Freud [1923] 1984: 381)), there is a crucial difference that leads to the opposition between sex and death. The death instinct (perhaps the term 'death wish' is apt here) 'rushes forward so as to reach the final aim of life as swiftly as possible. . .' The life instinct 'jerks back to a certain point to make a fresh start and so prolong the journey' (Freud [1920] 1984: 313). As such, sex/Eros is linked with the life instincts, being that 'which seeks to force together and hold together the portions of living substance' ([1920] 1984: 334), while the death instinct is found in the pull towards dissolution and fragmentation. The struggle between these instincts takes place in the id (Freud [1923] 1954: 401).

As we shall see, the death instinct and the way it is rendered innocuous by the libido has a particular impact upon Freud's account of society. However, the crucial role of death in the composition of the self requires that we pause a moment. The unconscious recognition of death is the ruling principle in Freud's account. Even the role given to Eros is predicated on the notion that all animate life is destined to become inanimate, to fall back into a previous way of being. Yet while the role of death may be prioritized, we should not attempt to oversimplify and thus distort Freud's account of the death instinct by eradicating the significance of eros. This is, I would suggest, the chief problem with Jonathan Dollimore's interpretation of Freud's position, offered in his *Death, Desire and Loss in Western Culture* (1998). While at one point Freud *does* claim that 'the aim of all life is death' (Freud [1920] 1984: 311), there is considerably more subtlety to this position than Dollimore will allow. Notions of fragmentation and dissolution do haunt the developing subject; but, at the same time, the desire for *extension and renewal* dominates the construction of one's sexuality.

Clarification of the power of the death instinct is found in Lacan's account of the mirror stage in childhood development. Lacan's version of the development of the ego focuses on the child aged between six and eighteen months. According to Lacan, the child sees its mirror image, and begins to formulate the idea that, in some way, that image is equatable with his or her self. However, the child's experience of life 'outside the mirror' is that it has limited control over the body that it sees represented in the mirror; the child is still dependent upon adults for his food, security and comfort. While he may have limited control over his own movements, before the mirror he finds 'the would-be autonomy and mastery of the individual in their earliest draft form' (Bowie 1991: 21–2). For Lacan this is not a moment of triumph: in locating the ego in the mirror, the child sets out on 'his career of delusional ego-building' (Bowie 1991: 24).

It is at this point that the power of the death instinct informs Lacan's account. For the child, the body seems out of control; it is, if you like, all over the place, and one only has to watch a child of this age to understand what Lacan is getting at. The apparent calmness and control of the mirror image dominates the creation of the ego, and in adulthood the individual will recall with horror the sense of disintegration associated with the lack of bodily control that characterizes those years. Evidence for this claim might be found in the fascination with horror felt in contemporary fiction and film. Images of dismemberment and putrification dominate this genre. Such features horrify us, not only because they remind us of our inevitable end; primarily they horrify because they remind us of our childhood experience of a body which is out of control, thus revealing the fiction of the autonomous self.

This recognition of the illusion of control, suggested by Lacan, can be linked to Freud's account of the power of the drive for dissolution. The illusion of the self is based upon the unconscious pull of the death drive, and the horror associated with the recognition that death is as much a part of our experience as life. In such a setting, it is not surprising that the very reality of bodily existence should elicit a sense of dread, and it is this dread which translates itself into a resistance to the anal, and, ultimately, to the rejection of sex itself. Becker calls such resistance 'the terror of living with a body' (Becker 1973: 164), and we shall return to these ideas later in this chapter. Yet for our purposes it is the attempt to reject the fundamental facts of human existence which all too often provides the foundation for spirituality. Indeed, when one reads accounts of ascetics drinking vomit, or licking sores (Bynum 1987), one is confronted, not with a celebration of the body, but by an attempt to transcend it by wallowing in its horrors. The ascetic challenges the primacy of bodily functions, and as a result emphasizes that which is truly significant: the soul. Yet what Freud points out is that the repression of the instinctual is not simply at work in the development of human systems of spirituality.[11] In developing society, according to Freud's theory, repression of the instinctual will also play a key part.

Society and the repression of the instinctual

Like that of Aristotle, Freud's account of the self is based upon the idea that there is an overriding purpose to human life. Like Aristotle, Freud equates this purpose with the desire for happiness. However, there is a difference. For Aristotle, true happiness (*eudaimonia*) could be achieved only through balancing the different desires one has for one's life, and to this end the exercise of reason is of paramount importance (Aristotle 1955). For Aristotle, it is thus at least possible that one might attain true happiness. Freud's account is ultimately different, and more pessimistic. His focus lies with what he calls 'the pleasure principle', which aims 'on the one hand, at an absence of pain and unpleasure, and, on the other, at the experiencing of strong feelings of pleasure' (Freud [1929] 1975: 13). In this sense, if we are to achieve pleasure, we must eradicate pain. Different methods might be employed to avert suffering; and, as Freud discusses intoxication, academic prowess, asceticism, love and aesthetics ([1929] 1975: 20), one senses the Aristotelian claim that none of these can give us the happiness we desire.

At this point the role of society in forming the individual becomes vitally important for Freud, for it suggests a way of finding happiness, although ultimately it can never deliver on its promise. Even as apparently optimistic a work as *The Future of an Illusion* (1927) reveals Freud's ambivalence on this issue. Here, Freud suggests that the dissolution of religion would prepare the ground for human happiness. However, while commenting that 'that would be the golden age', he goes on to say that 'it is questionable if such a state of affairs can be realized' (Freud [1927] 1985: 185). The role of society highlights this ambivalence. Freud argues that the desire to eradicate pain is a prime motivating force for the development of society, which in turn stems from the human fear of nature. We find ourselves placed in a physical environment that is neither friendly nor responsive to our desires. Indeed, our situation is so perilous that we fear that nature will destroy us. Thus we need to place a barrier between our selves and nature which suggests that in some way we are not part of the natural world order. The development of religion can be traced to a similar desire: we seek to give nature a friendlier, more human face, and thus 'God/gods' are developed with whom we can bargain (Freud [1927] 1985).[12]

Not surprisingly, then, if a civilized society is to develop, it is necessary that the instinctual life be repressed. Civilization is thus understood as that which stands in opposition to the natural world. The instincts reveal to us our true nature: that we are animals, rather than gods, and that, just as animals can be crushed by nature, so can we. Moreover, if we are to live in community, these primal urges must be controlled. In his paper '"Civilized" sexual morality and modern nervous illness' ([1908] 1985) Freud suggests that, the more civilized a society becomes, the more regulation is applied to the sex act. Ultimately this regulation culminates in a society where the only legitimate sex is for the purpose of reproduction (Freud [1908] 1985: 41). With good justification, Herbert Marcuse argues that Freud 'establishes a correlation between progress and increasing guilt feeling' (Marcuse [1956] 1987: 78). Yet this account of a society that increases the sense of frustration and guilt the more 'civilized' it becomes betrays a tension in Freud's account. Why would humans embrace civilization/society if to do so means relinquishing one of the basic means of attaining pleasure? If Freud's account is to make sense, there have to be good reasons for resisting/repressing an unfettered sexuality in favour of an ordered life in society. Marcuse argues that Freud is ultimately pessimistic: he cannot imagine a society in which the sex instincts are liberated. Marcuse may well have a point. It seems that, despite Freud's emphasis on those elements which connect us to the animal world, he is just as pessimistic about embodied existence as his predecessors in the Christian tradition. The body, so obviously associated with the physical world, is susceptible to the mutability of nature, and is thus to be feared. Sex, itself such a strong indicator of the connection between humans and animals, will have to be controlled if the control over nature is to be achieved.

The suppression of the sex instinct is problematic for the pursuit of pleasure, and thus for the achievement of happiness. By restricting sexual activity, anxiety about life and the fear of death arise (Freud [1908] 1985: 55). It is not readily apparent as to why Freud makes this connection. Perhaps it is because the restriction of sex leads us to develop other interests and ideas, which themselves suggest that we are not animals destined to die, but immortals who will survive the death of the physical body. Perhaps the nagging doubt remains that this is not the case, that despite all our best efforts we are no better than beasts in the field, and that our fate is no different from theirs. We are ambivalent creatures. Whatever, there is no doubt that, for Freud, while society might help us initially in our struggle with nature, ultimately its rule contributes to our misery.

Not only sex but also the death instinct must be repressed if a civilized society is to survive. Here, Freud focuses on the death instinct as that which seeks to destroy, which seeks a return 'to the quiescence of the inorganic world' (Freud [1920] 1984: 336). If society is to survive, the desire for destruction and violence must be rigorously controlled. Likewise, the denial of death must be maintained, as this mechanism enables people to behave as part of a community, rather than as individuals.[13] Adapting Dostoyevsky, 'if there is death, then all is permitted.' As society regulates sex and denies death, war becomes an interesting phenomenon, for it shatters the attempt to deny death's reality. While on one level death might be accepted as 'natural, undeniable, and unavoidable' (Freud [1915a] 1985: 77), on another we remain convinced of our own immortality – not in the sense that we will go on to a further existence after death, but in the sense that we will never die in the first place! Like Tolstoy's Ivan Ilyich, death is viewed as a chance event, an accident that can be avoided (Tolstoy [1886] 1981: 44). War challenges this neat assumption, especially if we are the ones in the thick of the battle.

Freud's discussion of the way in which these instincts are repressed in the attempt to structure society reveals something of the complexity of his approach. The difficulty of defining 'Eros' in the sense that Freud uses it in his later work is much in evidence. On the one hand, it is tempting to define it as the sex instinct that has to be repressed. However, it is Eros that attempts the construction of society against the pull of the death instinct (Marcuse [1956] 1987: 108), thus leading to a more complex account of Eros as 'the great unifying force that preserves all life' (Marcuse [1956] 1987: 27). The relationship between life/eros/sex and death is thus a complex and difficult one to define. Freud suggests that while these instincts are not diametrically opposed, they cannot simply be equated. Human life thus consists, in some sense, of a struggle between the sex/life and death instincts. Yet the complexity of the relationship between the two must not be ignored. Consider the following examples. The death instinct's aggression, while capable of destruction, is also used by the sex instinct: hence Freud's discussion of the way in which the death instinct is externalized in sadism or internalized in masochism (cf. Freud [1905] 1977: 70–73). Similarly, while at times Freud argues that both drives are inherently conservative, seeking to pull the individual back to the indistinctness of pre-organic life, at others he suggests that there is a difference even here. The death instinct always seeks to pull *the individual* back to the primordial state, and thus is termed 'the death *wish*' in 'Beyond the Pleasure Principle'. Eros, meantime, struggles for self-preservation, ultimately through the perpetuation of the species. Human society is thus constructed out of two conflicts: that between the instincts and that between the human individual and the natural world. It is this second conflict which must concern us now, for in shaping a spirituality based upon the facts of our human existence we need to consider those elements which have been resisted when constructing an account of humanity as a little lower than the angels.

Anality and the concept of 'man'

The Western concept of 'man' has developed through a series of similar philosophies, separated by time, but not necessarily by content.[14] As we have seen, Plato makes a distinction between the body and the soul, which constitutes the essential self. Descartes' thought is in many ways a development of Plato's: the self is established as a thinking thing, providing the bedrock for his epistemology. The body, by way of contrast, is seen as less real than the mind, in the sense that its existence cannot be established with the same certainty with which Descartes establishes the mind's existence. This dualistic account of the self is developed further in the Enlightenment philosophies of Kant and Hegel, where the human self is defined primarily by the ability to reason. Indeed, in all these philosophies, it is the ability to exercise the mind that differentiates humanity from the animal world.[15] This suggests that the dominant thinkers who have shaped the Western account of 'man' have largely ignored the basic physicality of human beings or, at best, have seen physicality as less significant than mental capability. Indeed, as was suggested in the previous chapter, even as self-consciously radical a movement as Sartrean existentialism ultimately locates human value and meaning in the phenomenon of consciousness. Fundamental to this account of the human self is the claim that human beings have the potential to transcend the physical world through the ability to reason. It is this 'transcendent quality' of the mind that leads Aristotle to the conclusion that the mind can survive the dissolution of the body.[16] Yet this understanding of the transcendental quality of 'man' has not been achieved without considerable struggle. This is not surprising, given the ambivalent, even contradictory, facts about human nature: we are 'half animal, half symbolic' (Becker 1973: 26). Our symbolic nature, fostered by society, brings us out of the natural world which we fear; yet, despite this, we are still mortal, still 'food for worms' (Becker 1973: 26).

It is this sense of the conflict between the mind/ideal and the body/physical that will be explored in this section by recourse to an aspect of our animality that, psychoanalytic theorists argue, underpins ideas and fears of both sexuality and mortality. Ernest Becker has offered a systematic exploration of this oft-neglected feature of our humanity: anality. It is this feature that challenges what might be termed the 'high', rather idealized, theories of selfhood outlined above. Not only does the anus represent the fact that we are tied to the body, it also represents the fate of all physical things: 'decay and death' (Becker 1973: 31). Philippe Ariès has written that 'decomposition is the sign of man's failure' (Ariès 1976: 42), and if we explore this idea we get some sense of the problem which defecation poses for the view that human beings are transcendent minds, separate from the change and flux of the physical world. The need to expel waste suggests that we cannot altogether transcend the basic facts surrounding our physicality. In this sense, the ideal of transcendent man is doomed to failure. Despite our ability to construct incredible, even beautiful, intellectual systems, we, like all other physical creatures, are limited by our bodily needs.

In similar vein, sex reminds us of our animal nature; but it has a further, more intimate connection with anality. Sexuality has invariably been connected with the lower part of the body, and, in this sense, has been viewed in conjunction with excretion and decay. In the following chapter we will consider the way in which the Marquis de Sade eroticizes defecation, suggesting a possible way of responding to the challenge anality makes to our sense of selfhood. More often, the problematic nature of sexuality has been supported through reflection on the anus. We are born 'between urine and faeces' – conceived there too – and there has been a strong trend in Western thinking that has tended to link sexuality with uncleanness and decay (cf. Power 1995:

44–9). This connection has had a considerable impact upon the way in which women and their experiences have been excluded from the formulation of ideals of humanity. Not only are humans born between urine and faeces; they are also born between the urine and faeces *of women*. This may seem insignificant, but consideration of this fact goes some way to explaining the exclusion of certain features of our humanity from the construction of the concept 'man'. The physical processes of reproduction are more obviously identifiable with the female body. Menstruation, pregnancy, birth and lactation all point to a less cerebral reality that is just as significant for understanding our humanity as is the activity of the brain. The rather limited role men have in reproduction has allowed male theorists to distance themselves from this process, and, in formulating their doctrine of 'man', women and their experiences have invariably been omitted. This has left the Western construct of 'man' reflecting a rather limited and disembodied account of the 'essential' self. It is significant that the dominant theorists of the self in the pre- and post-Enlightenment traditions have focused on rationality, thought, will, freedom and autonomy as the defining marks of human selfhood. These features distinguish us from the rest of the animal world, and are thus almost exclusively reflected upon when defining humanity. Features that connect us with the animal world – birth, sex and death – are invariably excluded, or confined to discussions of ethics rather than selfhood. It is interesting to note that, when a feature such as death is included within discussions of human selfhood, the emphasis is almost entirely upon formulating an account of mortality as something that can be transcended. The desire to transcend death is not limited to religious conceptualizing of a hereafter: we have seen how even humanistic/atheistic creeds such as Sartrean existentialism, which deal explicitly with death, suggest ways in which it can be transcended, either in the here and now or through the immortal nature of the written word.

Recent feminist theorizing has sought to redress the imbalance posed by the privileging of male experience in the construction of the self. Grace Jantzen has argued that the Western doctrine of the self is inadequate, precisely because of the paucity of reflection upon the fact that we are born (Jantzen 1998). Jantzen goes on to offer natality as an alternative paradigm for mortality when considering the nature of the human self. Christine Battersby, similarly, wishes to reflect upon the meaning of birth when formulating her account of the human person. As such, she starts from the pregnant female body, arguing that the ability of the human/female body to make space for another individual suggests something profound about the flexibility of human personhood (Battersby 1998). The rigidity of (male) theorizing on the self is thus exposed by contemplation of the female body and its processes.

Reflection upon the difference between mainstream (dare one say, male) accounts of the self and more recent feminist theorizing leads to the need for further discussion of the role given to sex and death in the Freudian account of the self. Ernest Becker, reflecting upon and developing Freud's ideas, suggests that the fear of the body underlies the problematizing of sex and death in the Western tradition. Feminist analysis takes us further: the connection made between sex and death may reflect the problem of physicality, but this 'problem' has been versed primarily through the male concerns and constructs of Western culture. Analysis of Becker's own arguments surrounding sex and death and their connection with anality may prove enlightening here.

At the heart of Becker's account of the denial of death lies a fundamental mistrust of the body. Adopting a dualistic account of the self, Becker suggests that human beings are caught between two aspects of their humanity: the ability to transcend their limited physical space, and the knowledge that they are, at root, animals. With Freud, Becker sees society as the attempt to control 'the mysterious processes of nature as they manifest themselves within his [sic] own body' (Becker 1973: 32). So, Becker argues, reflection upon the taboos surrounding menstruation, and the 'privacy' accorded to the rituals surrounding defecation, reveal the attempt to suppress the reality of our animality. Yet even at this early stage in his argument one senses that the problem he is dealing with may be a peculiarly male one. Menstrual taboos seem to have been placed *upon* women, not designed by women (Shuttle and Redgrove 1986). A good example of this might be the Victorian notion that the virtuous/feminine woman fainted at the sight of blood – a notion that seems somewhat bizarre given the fact of the monthly bleed, and which seems more likely to reflect a learnt response concerning what is expected of femininity in a particular society. Not surprisingly, both Becker and Freud miss a fundamental aspect concerning the way in which the body is suppressed. That is, it is not simply a case of *any* body being problematized: the fear of the mutability and animality of the body is projected onto women, who in turn are identified with those aspects of humanity which relate to physicality. Thus women are identified not only with sex, but also with death.

The ambivalence felt towards the mother in Becker's account underlines this identification. If Freud focuses his attention on the role played by the father at the expense of the mother, Becker provides a more detailed outworking of the problems posed by the maternal body, which should be placed in the context of the psychoanalytic debate regarding the respective roles of mother and father. Freud's dispute with Otto Rank over which is more important in developing the self is particularly significant. For Rank, birth trauma (and thus the role of the mother) are most significant, while for Freud it is the Oedipus complex (and thus the role of the father) which features most strongly in the development of human personality. As Peter Gay has noted, Freud's account is at odds with his own relationship with his parents (Gay 1995: 470ff), Freud's mother being the most influential figure in his childhood. This may, of course, suggest a different way of interpreting the Oedipus complex, where the primary role is given to the mother as love object, rather than the father as potential castrator. Be that as it may, Becker's concern is to show that the mother must be rejected if the self is to be appropriately established. According to Becker, fear of the mother arises from the realization that she is immersed in the body and its processes. Womanhood is thus identified with nature and the mortality of human flesh; the development into manhood requires escape from the female body (Becker 1973: 85). It seems relevant to ask whether women experience the body as quite the problem that Becker suggests it to be for men, who, in his thought, quickly become equated with humanity as a whole. The process of menstruation may suggest a different relationship with the body: perhaps the awareness that we are mutable beings, constantly changing. Possibly the menstrual cycle with its similarity to the lunar cycle suggests a connection between oneself and the physical processes of the natural world. Perhaps the female experience of orgasm suggests a similar awareness of the changing nature of the body, and of our place in the wider universe.[17] It should be noted that, even when the female body is considered negatively by feminist theorists, notably Beauvoir, such views are predicated upon a fundamental acceptance that, like it or not, we are identifiable with our bodies. Becker's account suggests a more problematic, possibly Platonic, reading of sex:

> Sex is an inevitable component of man's confusion over the meaning of his life, a meaning split hopelessly into two realms – symbols (freedom) and body (fate). (Becker 1973: 44)

Moreover, he writes that 'sex is of the body, and the body is of death' (Becker 1973: 162). This runs a similar course to Freud: for Becker the sex and death instincts are connected, yet different, and he suggests that sex represents 'species consciousness', the desire to maintain the life of the species rather than that of the individual. Women, as bearers of children, seem implicitly to be connected with sex and the species. However, for much of Becker's argument there is the desire that the individual should stand out from the species, and this will involve the suppression of sexuality. Indeed, as Becker puts it: 'resistance to sex is resistance to fatality' (Becker 1973: 164). One cannot help but draw the conclusion that the resistance to sex is also the resistance to woman.

Indeed, in Freud's work this connection between women, sex and death is tacitly admitted. In his essay 'The theme of the three caskets' (1913) the connection is made between women and death, and the mention is made of male desire to control both. In this essay, Freud takes two scenes from Shakespeare: the suitor's choice between three caskets in *The Merchant of Venice*, and King Lear's choice between his three daughters. Freud suggests that the two scenes mirror a common theme: in each, a man is being asked to choose between three women. His reasoning in the case of the example drawn from *The Merchant of Venice* seems to be that the caskets are 'vessels', a familiar archetype for the female. Freud focuses on what the third woman (Cordelia and the lead casket) represents. He feels that Cordelia's 'silence' and the 'paleness' of the lead suggest that in each case a woman is being linked with death (cf. Freud [1913] 1985: 238–40). Indeed, he goes further: the third woman is the goddess of death, and therefore it is possible to conclude we are dealing with the third figure in the trinity of the Fates/Moerae/Parcae/Norns: Atropos, 'the inexorable' ([1913] 1985: 241).

However, Freud's analysis does not stop there: not only are we dealing with the goddess of death in these examples; we are also dealing with the goddess of love. Indeed, in both the examples drawn from Shakespeare, the main issue revolves around love. The question posed in *The Merchant of Venice* ('who is to love Portia?') is similar to that asked in *King Lear* ('who loves Lear best?'). Freud finds this connection fascinating: why should the goddess of death be also the goddess of love? His answer lies in the realm of wish-fulfilment: in both cases, death is transformed into a beautiful, winnable woman, and thus we are left with the sense that death can be overcome, it can be controlled, it is not necessarily the end. In many ways, Freud is simply recognizing the connection between love and death in ancient mythologies. For example, Persephone is abducted and raped by the god of the underworld, Pluto/Hades. Yet she is not simply a 'victim'; she is also queen of the underworld, and thus has power over death. For Freud, the explanation for making this connection between death and a woman is simple: man is overcoming death by force of will, turning the uncontrollable reality of death into the controllable person of a beautiful woman. Yet, as Freud wryly notes, this can only ever be a form of wish-fulfilment. However, there is a sense in which Freud goes some way to explaining the patriarchal desire to control woman. On a practical level, controlling a woman's sexuality ensures legitimate offspring; on a symbolic level, controlling woman holds out the fiction of controlling death itself.

Conclusion: a spirituality of transience

Freud's work suggests a powerful connection between sex and death that ultimately draws the masculinist construction of woman into its analysis. In seeking to control woman and the sexuality associated with her, there is the suggestion that perhaps man can control his own mortality. Of course, Freud is at pains to point out that such desires are wish-fulfilments, but the very fact that this connection is made suggests something of the way in which the preoccupation with sex and death reflects a specific (patriarchal) construction of both masculinity *and* humanity. This is not to say that this is the only reading possible of these two features. Indeed, reflection on Freud's grappling with death holds a potential solution to the problem of human mortality for a spirituality that takes its reality seriously. While Freud's emphasis on the animalistic nature of humanity may seem antagonistic to the very possibility of a spiritual response to the world, this need not necessarily be the case. Indeed, his brief reflections on the problem of transience suggest an alternative approach to human spirituality based not upon a transcendent possibility which distances us from this world, but upon a form of transcendence based upon the values that can be derived from mutable human existence. By accepting our connection with the physical world, it may be possible to find a new depth and beauty for humanity.

Freud seems to have been obsessed with ageing and death from his mid-forties onwards. The death of his daughter Sophie during the 1920 influenza epidemic was a particularly painful and difficult blow for him to bear.[18] It is tempting to conclude that the emphasis on death in his development of psychoanalytic theory stems from the grief of this time (cf. Gay 1995: 394–95); yet this is an interpretation which Freud himself fiercely resisted. Whatever the truth of the matter, the extent to which thoughts of death preoccupied him from this point on seems wholly understandable. Since he was an atheist,[19] one might expect this obsession with death to translate into fear of death. This does not, however, appear to have been the case. In confronting his own painful death from cancer, he showed considerable courage, dying 'with dignity and without self-pity' (Gay 1995: 651).

This stoicism in the face of death suggests, at the very least, that Freud had in some way come to terms with his final destiny. Indeed, it is interesting to note that, amid his work on death and its problematic nature for 'man', there is an alternative, more positive attitude to the fact of mortality. The essay 'On transience' (1916) suggests that the desire to transcend this human realm may not be the only way in which humanity can imbue life with meaning. Freud details a conversation with a young friend who was depressed by the transience of natural beauty (Freud [1916] 1990: 287). How can we find meaning in a world which is constantly in the process of change, in which all that is around us is mutable and subject to decay? Freud disputes this pessimistic attitude to the natural world: 'a flower that blossoms only for a single night does not seem to us on that account less lovely' ([1916] 1990: 288). It has been suggested that this 'trite response' was simply a mischievous, possibly ironic, response to an earnest young man (Dollimore 1998: 181). But what if, rather than dismissing these reflections, we took them seriously? We have already noted the use of story and myth-making in Freud's psychoanalytic theory: at the very least, this suggests a place for a more poetic insight than that with which he is usually credited. If we follow through these reflections, might it not be possible to accept the reality of our animality/mortality, and still find meaning and beauty in life? My intention in the remainder of this book is to argue just this: that by accepting our grounding in this world we can form a spirituality based upon the value of human existence, rather than on a set of values imposed upon us from some transcendent horizon. In this sense, sexuality and mortality will not be considered aberrations to be overcome in formulating our account of humanity; on the contrary, these features of human existence will be placed at the centre of any formulation about human beings that we make.

Before defining such an account of human meaning and spirituality, it is important that we do not gloss over the difficulties of constructing an account of humanity that resists the claim that only a transcendent spirituality can endow human life with meaning. If we accept the reality of our sexualized selves, if we accept that we must all die, that there is no immortal future for us, are we left with no option but to accept the morally bereft universe illustrated so powerfully – and nauseatingly – in the works of the Marquis de Sade? According to Sade, in such a universe there are only libertines and victims; the libertine lives for and by sexual desire, and the greatest sexual pleasure is derived from the death of the victim/other. Is it possible to accept, like Freud, the fundamental animality of humanity without also accepting Sade's hell-like vision of the world?

4

Sex and Death in a Meaningless Universe: The Marquis de Sade

Introduction

We have reached the crux of the issue as far as any attempt to base a meaningful life upon the fundamental facts of the human condition is concerned. If we accept the view of humanity so eloquently described by Freud in the last chapter – that is, that we are creatures who reproduce through sexual intercourse (which, of course, has its own pleasures) and who are destined to die – are we committed to accepting a fundamentally meaningless and thus valueless universe? Freud suggests that there is beauty and a kind of meaning to be found in such mutability; but there is an alternative interpretation open to us if we accept with Freud that, despite the glories of human civilization, we are basically animals. If the world is emptied of transcendent meaning, there seems to be no reason why we should not simply pursue our own desires to the fullest extent, regardless of what that means for those around us.

The most vociferous proponent of this position remains a highly controversial figure, despite the fact that his books were written in the eighteenth century. To some he is the 'Divine Marquis'; to others, he is an unspeakable villain and sex-criminal (Dworkin 1981). Donatien-Alfonse-François, the Marquis de Sade, is a figure of undoubted reputation, yet one whose work is rarely read in any great detail. For a discussion such as this, his is a hard presence to avoid, as he graphically illustrates the pitfalls of attempting to ground a system of meaning in the processes of the physical universe. Even the alternative account of transcendence derived from Freud in the previous chapter is ultimately dependent upon the physical features of the natural world, and thus is open to the challenge Sade presents. It should be noted that, despite the power of Sade's challenge, those who advance the need for alternative spiritualities grounded in this world are often loath to engage with his work. For example, in her recent book *Becoming Divine* (1998), Grace Jantzen advances the view that the Western tradition is 'necrophilic', and that this obsession with death leads to an over-emphasis on the significance of human mortality. In an attempt to focus our thoughts on life instead of death, she offers the model of natality. We are creatures who are born, and focusing on this fact leads Jantzen to the conclusion that a shift in paradigm from mortality to natality will result in a similar shift from death-dealing to life-affirming values. Jantzen appears, then, to make a clear-cut, almost Platonic, distinction between life and death and the values that can be derived from each. By polarizing these concepts, she seems to make a similar distinction between sex and death. Any discussion of death is invariably associated with male violence and destruction. Sex, by way of contrast, is associated with intimacy and the possibility of new life and experience. In this, Jantzen stands in a long tradition of feminist reclamation of the body and sexuality, seeing in such features the foundation for a feminist spirituality (cf. Isherwood and Stuart 1998). Such a conclusion might be challenged through an engagement with Sade, for in his writings it is far from clear that sexuality can be understood in such a straightforwardly positive manner. Indeed, in his writing a strong connection is made between sex *and* death. Jantzen, despite her concern to engage with the necrophilia of the tradition, does not refer to Sade's work at all. This is unfortunate, for I shall contend that it is through grappling with his ideas that we may arrive at a position that accepts our animality, but which is able to base real meaning and value in our humanity. This will involve a critical engagement with the nature of sexuality and embodiment, which in turn necessitates renewed consideration of the importance of mind or the reflective life (the aim of chapter 5). Sade presents us with the full horror of a universe deprived of all meaning, where all that matters is physical pleasure. I shall argue that we do not need to facilitate a return to an external moral order to combat Sade's vision; rather, by subverting aspects of

Sade's own thesis, we can go some way to developing a meaningful vision of human existence, grounded in the experience of being human in this world. In this chapter we move a step closer to a spirituality that includes the immanent and transcendent qualities derived from reflection upon what it means to be human.

The Sadeian universe

Sade presents his reader with a world of stark brutality, a world where pleasure is invariably linked with sexual acts which almost always involve some kind of violence and even death. His 'libertines', committed to an ideal of total freedom, pursue their desires to the extreme, regardless of the number of victims this creates. In Sade's writing there is an inevitable escalation of violence, each of his major novels culminating in some hideous scenario of death.[1] Yet despite the dubious literary worth of his novels, and the fact that the acts he details can be found in other works of pornography, an apparently more serious intent informs his writing. Sade saw himself as a philosopher (Airaksinen 1995: 5–6) and accordingly viewed his novels as offering the reader a dramatic presentation of his own philosophy.

Nature versus God and reason

Sade's philosophy is based upon the rejection of any kind of transcendent moral order. It is important that the far-reaching nature of that rejection is grasped. It is not simply the rejection of a *theological* moral order based upon a transcendent God (cf. Sade [1787] 1992: 123);[2] Sade also rejects the notion that there could be a moral order based upon a high view of *human* being as distinct from the rest of the animal world. To this end, both God and reason (that which has traditionally been understood as distinguishing humanity from the animals) are critiqued and rejected. Humanity can be afforded no special status in the universe. So, in *Juliette*, Noirceuil argues that human being should be understood 'as something on the order of an absolutely material plant' (Sade [1797] 1968: 267); there is no difference between a human being and a vegetable. Both are created by Nature, both are simply material. In a later passage from the same novel,

Voldomir expresses a similar view, and goes on to show the impact that accepting this conclusion will have upon human relations:

> If it be true that we resemble all other products of Nature, if it be true we are worth no more than they, why persist in believing ourselves governed by different laws? Are plants and animals acquainted with mercy, pity, social obligations, brotherly love? And in Nature do we detect any law other than self-interest, that is self-preservation? (Sade [1797] 1968: 888)[3]

To take such claims seriously means the end of simplistic accounts of good and evil (in this sense, Sade presages Nietzsche). If there is no privileged position for humanity, then what happens to a human being is of no greater significance than what happens to a carrot, shredded to be consumed in a salad. This is what makes Sade such a frightening writer to read: and I would contend that, if we fail to find him terrifying, we have not read him properly.[4] Without a transcendent moral order, based on God, he presents a universe where being human does not secure any rights or obligations. There is no justice, only the 'natural' law of survival of the fittest/strongest.

There is, however, something of a tension in Sade's thought on this point. While he rejects both God and reason as guarantors of the moral order, his libertines frequently make use of both to advance their own pleasure. Reason, in the shape of philosophical dialogue, is invariably employed to destroy virtue. So, much of *Philosophy in the Boudoir* is concerned with recounting the arguments which Dolmancé and Saint-Ange use to convince Eugenie of the 'truth' of libertinage (Sade [1795] 1995). Similarly, the story of Juliette begins with the Abbess Delbène convincing the thirteen-year-old girl of the pointlessness of virtue in an amoral universe (Sade [1797] 1968: 12–20). Reason, it seems, can be employed to dethrone God and received notions of morality. Likewise, the God whose non-existence is constantly, even repetitively, proclaimed is used as the standard against which transgression can take place. So, the depraved Brothers of St-Mary-in-the-Wood dress Florette as the Virgin Mary and then give full vent to their passions which have been inflamed by the prospect of committing sacrilege (Sade [1791] 1990b: 612–13). It would seem that even Sade cannot pursue his vision to its logical end: even a libertine needs to believe that there is some transcendental quality to the universe if he is to experience the 'true' pleasure of transgressing those very values.

Leaving aside the tensions in Sade's thought for a moment, Sade replaces the transcendent God and the supremacy of reason by prioritizing Nature. In this he appears to follow the Romantics, who viewed the natural world as something with which we should unite, rather than something to be submitted to the eye of reason (cf. Tarnas 1991: 367). However, Sade differs from such writers by positing a less positive and more disturbing image of what, precisely, constitutes 'Nature'. Nature – or at least Sade's reading of what constitutes Nature – provides the blueprint for how we should act. Considering the ambivalent character of the natural world, it is not necessarily obvious which features will inform Sade's account. Given his proclivities, it is perhaps not surprising that he focuses on the brutal and the violent. There is a sense in which David Hume's famous picture of the amoral 'vivifying principle' which is Nature finds full expression in Sade's imagination (cf. Hume ([1779] 1947: 211). Thus, through Bressac, Sade says:

> Our acts of destruction give [Nature] new vigour and feed her energy, but none of our wreckings can weaken her power. So of what concern is it to Nature, endlessly creating, if a mound of flesh which today has the shape of a woman, should reproduce itself tomorrow as countless insects of different types? (Sade [1787] 1992: 40).

At least for Hume solace is to be found in the faculty of reason: Sade resists even that consolation. Nature is severe, brutal and destructive. An appreciation of the ecological cycle seems to underpin Sade's vision: the recycling of matter is what Nature is about, and Sade uses this understanding as the basis for his rejection of the sanctity of life. To murder is simply to allow 'exhausted matter [to] re-enter the regenerating womb'([1797] 1968: 770). By killing, the libertine is simply aiding Nature's ultimate goal. The move from a teleological system of value to a cyclical one has far-reaching implications for the nature of human action. For Sade, living in accordance with Nature is quite different from living in accordance with the will of God: to follow Nature means to enter into her destructive cycle.[5] Thus, the Pope tells Juliette that murder has no moral approbation attached to it: 'what can it matter if of a man I make a cabbage, a lettuce, a butterfly, or a worm . . .?' (Sade [1797] 1968: 773). In killing, one is simply accepting one of Nature's most basic laws.

It would, however, be too simplistic to see Nature as having a purely positive role in allowing the pursuit of all desires. There is, in fact, a more ambivalent relationship between Nature and her 'followers', the libertines, which Sade outlines. Nature is both friend and enemy of the libertine. She is friend, as she provides a rationale against which the libertine can support his actions; but even then Sade is at pains to portray 'the havoc of nature' (Sawhney 1994: 3). She is enemy, in much the same way that the mother is portrayed as enemy in Sade's stories (Gallop 1995). 'Mother Nature' has the ability to crush even the libertine, just as the mother represents the possibility of returning to the undifferentiated state of the womb.

Woman, sex and death

This leads to a further feature of Sade's universe. The female and the maternal are to be resisted; as Roland Barthes puts it, Sade is concerned with 'hiding the Woman' (Barthes 1977: 123). Bearing in mind Sade's explicit descriptions of sexual acts and orgies, the sex organs of the female participants are often covered, veiled or hidden.[6] Sometimes this desire to obliterate female alterity takes a brutal turn: the fate of Mme de Mistival in *Philosophy in the Boudoir* is perhaps the most disturbing of the acts Sade portrays (for some suggested reasons, see Barthes 1977: 169).[7] Come to rescue her daughter Eugenie, she becomes her daughter's victim: Eugenie, now thoroughly schooled in libertinage, takes a needle threaded with a waxy red cotton and stitches up her mother's vagina and anus. It is surely no coincidence that such a fate should await her: mothers and the maternal are consistently denigrated and abused in Sade's universe. Bressac in *The Misfortunes of Virtue*, who will eventually murder his mother, explains his desire to do so to Justine. He argues that there is no reason why one should respect one's mother as she plays no part in forming the child in the womb. Taking Aristotelian biology somewhat literally, he argues that only the father's seed 'creates' the child, thus to kill one's mother is no crime (especially as she 'no doubt' enjoyed the act which led to pregnancy in the first place!). Moreover, Bressac continues, he would 'never have raised my hand against my father' (Sade [1787] 1992: 41): after all, he is the real source of his existence. Similarly, in *120 Days of Sodom*, pregnancy is treated as a crime, as attested to by the fate of Constance, who, after hearing stories of the butchering of pregnant women (which, not surprisingly, distress her), is herself tortured and then murdered by her chief tormentor, Curval, who cannot bear the physical signs of her fertility: 'Curval himself opened Constance's belly and tore out the fruit, already well-ripened and clearly of the masculine sex' (Sade [1785] 1990a: 670).

Strangely, given the fertility of nature, it is precisely this feature of the natural world that Sade resists and finds repulsive. The cruelty meted out to mothers who reflect the fecundity of nature is mirrored by the fact that vaginal intercourse ('cunt-fucking') is seen by Sade's 'great' libertines as subordinate to anal sex ('bum-fucking'). This does not necessitate the conclusion that Sade is homosexual: it is notable that Juliette's position as a supreme libertine is to an extent based upon her contention that anal intercourse is more enjoyable than vaginal intercourse (Sade [1797] 1968: 430). (It may, of course, challenge the very notion that one can simply describe individuals as hetero- or homosexual.) But drawing attention to Juliette's sexual preferences is not tantamount to saying that Sade offers a view of sex that is liberating for women, or indeed that he is committed to the liberation of women outside the bedroom. Commentators such as Coward might argue that Sade is not particularly misogynistic: 'in Sade's world, obscenity and cruelty are the prerogative of the strong, irrespective of gender' (Sade [1787] 1992: xxvii). But careful analysis of the text reveals an over-arching attitude to women, and particularly female sexuality, which is far more complex.

At the heart of Sade's account of woman lies an ambivalence towards the female sexual organs. There is undoubtedly a shunning of the cunt in favour of intercourse that involves the anus. This may represent a misogyny grounded in the fear of female sexual organs. Witness, for example, the following exchange between two of Justine's tormentors:

> 'Look ye, friend,' said the younger, 'a girl's a pretty thing, eh? But what a shame there's that cavity there.'
> 'Oh!' cried the other, 'nothing nastier than that hole, I'd not touch a woman even were my fortune at stake.' (Sade [1791] 1990b: 631)

Such comments resonate with Sartre's discussion of the 'hole' that is feminine sexuality, and bring us to the heart of the matter. What is it about the female sexual organs that inspires this kind of revulsion and fear? Reflection on Sade may help us to get closer to an answer. In his work, the rejection of the cunt is undoubtedly connected to the horror of pregnancy and birthing. Pregnant women in Sade's universe serve no purpose other than to be mistreated and even murdered (cf. Sade [1797] 1968: 618–22). Even when not employed as a receptacle for the libertine's rage, the image of the womb is used to belittle the possibility of love between man and woman. The Comte de Belmor, in his speech against love, at one point uses the idea of birthing to diminish the possibility of any lasting affection for a woman: 'Picture her giving birth, this treasure of your heart; behold that shapeless mass of flesh squirm sticky and festering from the cavity where you believe felicity is to be found' ([1797] 1968: 510).

The 'stickiness' of the newborn child returns us to Sartre's account of femininity. There is no order attested to here; the infant is described as shapeless, formless. This may suggest something about the perceived 'chaos' associated with female sexuality: order has to be imposed from without; it is not an inherent aspect of the physical world. It has often been noted that Sade's universe is one peculiarly concerned with the ordering of sexual desire: the pleasure of the libertines is invariably associated with the idea that order should be introduced to the sexual act. Again, this suggests that the dismissal of reason as a key aspect of our humanity is not carried through to its logical conclusion in Sade's work. When the word 'festering' appears in the above passage we get an even clearer sense of the issues raised by the womb. Life, beginning in the womb, inevitably proceeds to the tomb. Such ideas resonate with those of Sartre, and a brief comparison of Sartre and Sade at this juncture reveals something of the ultimate concerns that drive masculinist discourse on the nature of human existence.

Sartre's philosophy, while rejecting God and a transcendent moral order, still offers an account of humanity that demands that we transcend the physical world. We are, remember, to 'create ourselves' by 'standing out' from the physical world. At first glance, Sade offers a radically different account of human life: throw yourself into the physical, finding in sexual pleasure the 'meaning' of life. However, Sade's emphasis on ordering sexual experience suggests that a form of transcendence is being offered, albeit one which is grounded in human activity rather than imposed upon it from without. In this sense, his account is similar to that offered by Sartre. And, again, similar views are offered by both when they turn their attention to the origins and destiny of human existence. Death remains the determining issue for both. Sartre is candid about the problems this fact poses: death renders life absurd. Sade comes at this issue from a different angle: his libertines invariably accept the idea that death marks the end of the human individual, but argue that to accept this fact is of no more moment than accepting one's non-existence prior to birth (Sade [1797]1968: 49).

Yet it is Sade's reflections on procreation that suggest these beliefs are not quite so secure as he would have his reader believe. As we have seen, characters such as Bressac argue that the mother provides nothing. And it is reflection on this 'nothing' that introduces his reader to ideas of annihilation and death. The mother provides 'no-thing',[8] and it is this absence of content that suggests the void to which we will be returned at death. The mother might give the child life, but it is a life framed by death. Rather than resembling life, she represents the inevitability of death that comes with entering into the natural cycle of the physical world. Indeed, Sade can be seen to give dramatic expression to such ideas in his descriptions of the murderous mothers Olympia and Juliette. Reflecting upon the murder of her daughter, Olympia concludes: 'I restored to the elements an inert mass which had received life in my womb only in order to become the toy of my rage and my viciousness' (Sade [1797] 1968: 714). There is an ambiguity about human existence that means that these words could be applied to any child born into the cycle of life and death. Against such a backdrop, the rage detailed by Sade against pregnant women can be understood as rage against the inevitability of death. The violence meted out to the female sex organs is simply a variation of the anger that knowledge of death brings. We are not immortal, and the realization of that fact leads to this outpouring of violence.

Sade's presentation of female libertines does somewhat mask the fact that it is the female that represents death in his universe. Camille Paglia might applaud his presentation of characters such as Juliette and Mme de Saint-Ange as 'high priestesses of savage nature' (Paglia 1991: 238); yet even she has to admit that he 'detests procreative women' (1991: 244). It is by reflecting upon this fact that we arrive at what drives Sade's imagination: revenge on the female and the mother.

It is at this point that we must turn our attention to the connection that he makes between sex and death. If Freud considers these features of human life in terms of two competing drives that are interrelated, Sade suggests an inseparable connection between the two. One of the most noteworthy features of Sade's writings is the extent to which the pleasure of the sexual act is ultimately grounded in the death of the other. This structure is clearly present in the story of Juliette. Juliette's entry into libertinage begins with fairly standard sexual practices: mutual masturbation ('frigging'), oral sex, vaginal sex and anal sex. But basing the meaning of one's life purely upon sexual encounters means that there is a constant need for something different, something which will excite the sated senses with its innovation. The dissatisfaction inherent in libertinage is alluded to by Juliette when she comments: 'the effect of irregular desires [is that] the greater the height they arouse us to, the greater the emptiness we feel afterward' (Sade [1797] 1968: 312). Rather than seek something outside such sexual acts to establish some kind of meaningful life, Juliette simply presses on with her attempts to find new and varied sexual acts. Soon, 'if there was not something exceptional or criminal in the frolics which were proposed to me, I could not even feign an interest in them' ([1797] 1968: 548). And it is this criminal element that necessitates the death of the other in order to secure ultimate pleasure in the sexual act. Sex and death quickly become linked in Sade's economy of desire. So Clairwil, while picking over the aftermath of one massacre, asks: 'think you one ever tires of the sight of death? Ever has enough of it? It was, to be sure, one of the most delicious horrors I've witnessed in all my days, but it is certain to leave me with an enduring sadness. For, alack, one cannot enjoy a massacre every fifteen minutes the whole length of one's life' (Sade [1979] 1968: 978).

Why should the death of the other excite the senses in this manner? At this point, perhaps we should reflect a little on *our own response as readers* to the acts that Sade presents. (Or, if these acts are too repellent, we might think about our response to cinematic representations of violence and death (cf. Carroll 1990).) What gives the representation of the death of the other its peculiar power to intrigue and excite? Returning to Sade's universe, possible answers present themselves. As we have noted, Sade's libertines are described as unconcerned by the fact of their own mortality. However, reflection on the role of the mother suggests that the inevitability of death remains a problem, albeit a problem which is repressed, but which finds expression through rage against the mother. Another, equally strong, response is to deproblematize death by romanticizing it (Dworkin 1981: 175). From being something that horrifies and repels, death is turned into something that has an artistic quality, a beautiful quality.[9] Notably, Roland's torture chamber, while including human victims, also contains the waxen image of a crucified woman, whose beautiful hair and face, disfigured by tears, is described by Justine (Sade [1791] 1990b: 673).

Treating death in this way suggests a control over it that we do not, in fact, possess, and thus reiterates Freud's comments on *The Merchant of Venice* and *King Lear,* where he argues that the attempt to control death is made by giving it the shape of a winnable woman.

It is this issue of control that ultimately informs Sade's approach to death. The death of the other always arises as a deliberate act perpetrated by the libertine. This gives the libertine a sense that death is under their control, that it is not as powerful as its inevitability might suggest. This point is emphasized by the way in which Juliette murders her closest 'friends' Olympia and Clairwil. There is a surprising suddenness in the way in which they are dispatched, which seems designed to replicate the unpredictability of death (Sade [1797] 1968: 1017; 1029–30). This literary conceit creates the false sense that even the randomness of death is under the libertine's control. This is highlighted by Roland's 'experiment' with hanging, which convinces him of the pleasure it is possible to feel when dying, and thus leaves him with no fear of death ([1797] 1968: 687–8) – an idea which is reiterated by Juliette ([1797] 1968: 1014). Even the libertine's own death will be pleasurable.

Despite his emphasis on cruel and violent deaths, Sade sidesteps the existential horror of death when it comes to considering the death of the subject. In noting Juliette's death, he does so in a vague and disingenuous way. Ten years after the events he details, he writes that: 'the death of Madame de Lorsange [Juliette] caused her *to disappear* from the world's scene, just as it is customary that all brilliant things on earth finally *fade away*' (Sade [1797] 1968: 1193; my emphasis). There is a peace, a tranquillity alluded to in her passing that was denied her victims, but which seems to represent the ideal for Sade. In seizing life by the throat, Juliette will find a similar control over her own death. Sade has effectively evaded the fear of the death in a way that is not altogether convincing – especially when one thinks of the passage where Juliette, prisoner of the thief Brisatesta, fears that she will suffer the same fate as her own victims ([1797] 1968: 807). She quickly masters this fear, and, of course, comes out of the experience unscathed and better off. But this allusion to her fear suggests that death is not so easily confronted as Sade would have us believe.

Consideration of the control Sade hopes to exercise over death may go some way to explaining an aspect of his work which seems most bizarre: the passion for coprophagy, or the eating of faeces. For some of his libertines, this is an act of supreme pleasure (cf. Sade [1785]

1990a: 371); the question of wherein the pleasure of this act might reside is more difficult to ascertain. Dworkin suggests that the issue of control is again of paramount importance: in this case, control over every aspect of the victim's life. She argues that this act provides the final feature of 'a sexuality which is entirely cannibalistic' (Dworkin 1981: 94). The victim has no control over their own life: power resides with the libertine who can make use of any part of the victim's body to attain their own pleasure.

There is much in Dworkin's analysis to commend it, but I would wish to contend that coprophagy makes more sense when placed alongside our previous discussion of the meaning derived from the death of the other. As was noted in the previous chapter, defecation, like death, reminds us of the transience of human life. Contrary to what the phenomenon of thought suggests, we are not gods, but animals. The eating of faeces suggests defiance in the face of a mutable universe. That which marks us as animals – the need to defecate – need not horrify us, but can be responded to with pleasure; in this instance, it can even give us sustenance. Reflection on this phenomenon may even suggest that Sade is seeking to find a way in which we might transcend nature. Indeed, his emphasis on what might be considered 'unnatural' acts suggests that it is through shaping sexuality that human beings are able to transcend the apparently inescapable lot of human being.

Undoubtedly Sade's work reveals something of the complexities of human sexuality. He reveals to us the dark side of human sexuality, where sex is associated with violence, force and coercion,[10] where the concern with order and control leads to power structures that necessitate the existence of master and slave, perpetrator and victim. When constructing a spirituality that includes sexual experience it is undoubtedly important to remember the ways in which sex can be used to the detriment of human persons, and reflection on Sade's universe challenges any simplistic attempt to reclaim the body and sexual experience. But sex does not always involve the kind of horrors that Sade details: it can also involve love, mutuality and respect. And perhaps it is through reflecting upon these features that a different kind of transcendence might be felt. As Sade suggests, we are not simply a prey to natural forces: we can create value and meaning. In this sense, transcendence and immanence need not be considered as polarized dualities, but rather as inclusive features of human life. We can reflect upon the experiences that we have, deriving from them ideas such as 'love', 'mutuality' and 'respect'. What remains to be seen is whether such an immanental form of transcendence can avoid the excesses that define the Sadeian universe.

Sade claims to describe a universe in which any kind of transcendent value is eradicated. The extent to which he can maintain this position, given his emphasis on the construction of sexuality, is debatable. Yet his attempt to destroy the transcendent leaves us with a particular set of issues that must be addressed if a this-worldly form of transcendence is to be advanced. The obliteration of transcendent value, according to Sade, results in a universe of horrors. We might initially feel that the only response is to seek refuge in a moral order imposed on the world from without – a rather different view of what constitutes the transcendent than that which I am seeking to advance. A return to 'good old God' (Lacan [1958] 1982: 140) might seem the only way of preserving justice and humanity in the face of a rapacious and unforgiving universe. This need not be the case. By pursuing our analysis of Sade's universe we shall, I contend, find that Sade himself provides the tools with which to subvert his claim that, if we reject the old securities of an ontologically distinct God or moral order, then we must accept the brutalizing features of life as he describes it.

Subverting Sade: meaning in a meaningless universe

The Society of the Friends of Crime

In Sade's universe the libertine does not necessarily act alone, and invariably is a member of a shadowy group known variously as 'the Sodality of the Friends of Crime' (*Juliette*), or the 'School for Libertinage' (*120 Days of Sodom*). Reflection upon the way in which such groups function holds the key to resisting Sade's vision, and the underlying supposition that, if an external moral order is rejected, 'anything goes'. It would seem that libertine 'society' is the basis for Sadeian practice. A good example is to be found by considering the four 'friends' who devise the four-month debauch that forms the basis for the action of *120 Days of Sodom*. They are bound together by a complex network of relationships: Blangis and the Bishop are brothers; Curval is married to Blangis' daughter Julie, Blangis to Durcet's daughter Constance, Durcet to Curval's daughter Adelaide. Yet when one considers the actual behaviour of the libertines, we quickly realize that there is no genuine relationship, society or friendship between these people. Affectionate relationships are ridiculed, and familial bonds exist only to be perverted: the fathers mentioned above all have incestuous relationships with their daughters. A similar trend is to be found in Sade's other novels: for example, Juliette is involved in the deaths of her father, sister and daughter. Barthes is undoubtedly correct when he notes that: 'sadian [*sic*] partners are neither comrades, chums, nor co-militants' (Barthes 1977: 133). When Sade portrays human relationship, he alludes to nothing that is positive or life-affirming: there is no mutuality, no shared experience, no laughter.

Indeed, isolation is the key feature of the Sadeian universe. The libertine is, despite his connection to such groups, a solitary figure who has no commitments, not even to other libertines. The possibility of friendship between libertines is a concept much discussed and debated by Sade's characters. Saint-Fond is at pains to argue against the feelings of friendship 'as empty, as illusory as love' (Sade [1797] 1968: 232). Self-seeking, self-aggrandizement and self-interest are for him the building blocks of human relationship, and thus he concludes that friendship cannot legitimately stand alongside such practices and ideals. Yet even this clear-cut conclusion is open to contradiction: Saint-Fond later comments: 'I shall never be treacherous toward my friends' ([1797] 1968: 481); although his reason for saying this is self-interested: 'one cannot very well do without something solid and sure in the world; and what's left if you cannot count upon your intercourse with your friends?' ([1797] 1968: 481–2).

Actions invariably speak louder than words, and Juliette's conduct suggests the dubious status accorded to friendship in Sade's universe. Despite her declarations of lasting friendship to both Olympia and Clairwil, her closest associates, Juliette is ultimately responsible for their deaths. Given this background, it is not surprising that the apparently lasting friendship she finds with Durand is subject to doubt: to what extent is it possible to place one's life in another's hands, especially when that other shares one's murderous designs? Sade resolves this tension by having Juliette undergo an ordeal devised by Durand to test the strength of her trust (Sade [1797] 1968: 1049–50): apparently this will prove conclusively that Durand will never harm her. Indeed, that is Juliette's own conclusion. But oaths of lasting friendship mean little in a universe ruled by self-interest and unbridled desire.

Ultimately, there is no real friendship in Sade's universe: even his libertines can become victims to one another. In a sense, Sade's libertine is

the logical outworking of the emphasis upon 'Man' as a free, autonomous, self-sufficient individual that emerges from the Western canon.
Sade apparently pushes this image as far as it will go, revealing the possible alienation from others that results from giving too much credence
to this account of the human self. There is no sense that the individual
might find their meaning in community or through relationship with
others. This becomes particularly clear when one considers the location
for Sade's dramas. The action of his stories invariably takes place in
remote, isolated places, where the protagonists and their victims are
deliberately distanced from ordinary human commerce. So, Sade describes at length the difficulties of arriving at the Chateau of Silling, the
backdrop for the events of *120 Days of Sodom* ([1785] 1990a: 235-6),
leading to the conclusion that, were the bridge to the chateau removed,
'there is not on this entire earth a single being, of no matter what species
you may imagine, capable of gaining this small plot of level land' ([1785]
1990a: 236–7). Such isolated spots reflect the alienation of human beings under Sade's worldview: Justine, with good reason, expresses her
dislike of 'all solitary places' ([1787] 1992: 108).

This sense of the isolated self is driven home when one considers the
nature of sex in the Sadeian universe. While an infinite number of
sexual acts are described (seemingly *ad nauseam*),[11] there is not a single example of Sade describing the touch or connection between those
engaged in these acts. There is no sense of intimacy; his readers are
simply presented with sexual acts expressed solely in terms of the specific bodily parts that these acts involve. In this way, the body is frag-
mented into a series of fetishisms that necessitates that individual
characters are described according to the merits of their individual
body parts (cf. Sade [1797] 1968: 1133). As a direct consequence, the
sex that he presents is de-eroticized: sex becomes a matter of engaging
with particular body parts, rather than creating intimacy between two
human beings. A good example is provided by Durand's contraption
that enables a father to possess the lower five-sixths of his daughter's
body without her knowing that he is her attacker (Sade [1797] 1968:
1134). The relationship between father and daughter may be destroyed
in this act, but when one reads the narrative one senses that both 'father' and 'daughter' have disappeared: there is simply a body here to
be beaten and sodomized, and an erection to be had. Describing the
body thus does not just affect individual relationships: it affects the
very possibility of human society: 'When face is averted from face,
emotion and society are annihilated' (Paglia 1991: 246).

Sade may claim to base his philosophy upon the physicality of being human, but his ideas are inspired by a more traditional understanding of what makes us human. Sade's account of the body is informed by a far-reaching dualism that sees the body as simply matter to be used, abused and destroyed. What matters in Sade's universe is not physical connection, but the way in which *ideas* can be put into practice. Despite the apparent radicalism of his philosophy, the body remains subservient to the mind.

This intellectualization of the body and sexuality is inadvertently maintained by Sade's modern admirers. For example, Camille Paglia in her discussion of Sade is at pains to remind her reader, who might be horrified by the excesses Sade details, that 'these are ideas, not acts' (Paglia 1991: 242). A distinction is drawn between thoughts/ideas and acts/reality. Mind and body/physicality are thus distinguished, and this enables her to mitigate the cruelty of Sade's system. She draws him as a radical thinker, whose intention is to break down traditional hierarchical values through his muddling of gender and familial roles. Indeed, Sade consistently plays with gender roles and familial ties. Thus Eugenie, while raping and sodomizing her mother in *Philosophy in the Boudoir*, exclaims: 'Here I am: at once incestuous, adulterous, sodomistic; and all that in a girl who only shed her maidenhead today!' (Sade [1795] 1995: 147). Paglia takes such ideas and makes Sade a liberating figure, whose assault on human relationships challenges oppressive social structures and moral norms.

A similar intellectualization is at work when Sade's apologists turn their attention away from his literary corpus to his real-life crimes. There is an attempt to downplay the assaults perpetrated by Sade on poor women and prostitutes, so that what happened to these women was not really so awful and therefore does not overly matter. Andrea Dworkin has effectively analysed the way in which this happens in the writings of the intelligentsia who act as apologists for Sade (Dworkin 1981: 80–88). In particular, she draws attention to the implicit gender politics informing such arguments: 'What happens to men is portrayed as authentic, significant, and what happens to women is left out or shown not to matter' (1981: 80).

It is interesting to note that even those with a Marxist perspective, which, one supposes, would lead them to identify with the oppressed, seek to absolve Sade by considering his crimes against the backdrop of the society from whence he came. So Stephen Pfohl writes: 'Sade's crimes never exceeded the institutionally condoned violence of aristo-

cratic and early bourgeois men against both women and the poor'
(Pfohl 1994: 26).[12]

But this point begs the question. If *Pfohl* had been Rose Keller –
abducted, beaten, threatened with death if she tried to escape – would
it really matter to him if that level of violence was no greater than that
perpetrated by others at the time? A deceit is being employed when
intellectuals seek to excuse Sade's acts in this way that betrays their
bias: ultimately the woman/prostitute/victim is less significant than
the man of letters. To put it another way, Sade's 'mind'/ideas excuse
his acts. Bizarrely, bearing in mind the fact that many of his apologists
seek to reject the Cartesian dualism which underpins Western society,
they themselves espouse a dualist position. Innovative ideas (the male
mind) are prioritized over acts (the female body).

This structure may go some way to explaining the peculiarity of the
Sadeian text. Anyone who comes to Sade expecting the simplicity of
much pornography will be sorely disappointed, as a great deal of his
narrative consists of long, involved dialogues about the meaning of
existence. Moreover, the very basis of libertinage itself is located in
the workings of the mind. Juliette's advice to Donis, concerning the
ways of heightening pleasure, underlines this point. Deciding upon
one's desires involves calm reflection: 'let it be your head and not your
temperament that commands your fingers' (Sade [1797]1968: 640).
Of paramount importance is 'the idea' ([1797] 1968: 640), which,
once fixed upon, is to be written down, edited and embellished. Sade's
great libertines consistently demand that one acts not out of the passions, but with a coolness that will heighten one's pleasures. True libertinage demands the prioritization of mind over body, and it is this
dualism that inevitably influences the dualism that develops in his account of human relationship, where the only subject is the libertine,
and all others are objectified as potential victims. It also suggests that,
despite his protestations, he is offering a transcendental account of the
self. My mind can transcend/shape my physical responses/desires. So,
when faced with rape I can either enjoy the experience and become a
libertine, or hate it and become a victim. What matters is how I *respond* to such experiences.[13]

Sade, then, shows how Western individualism, taken to its logical
conclusion, can result in the destruction of human relationship. Sade
presents a view of human relationship mediated through an almost
Hegelian dualism of oppressed and oppressor, libertine and victim.
Clearly, there are situations in the world that reflect such hierarchical

relationships, and, as Martha Nussbaum notes, Lucretius' attack on sexual love has precisely this form of sexual relationship in its sights (Nussbaum 1994a: 140–191).[14] Yet these are by no means the only ways of considering how human relationships or even human society might function. Sade resists any claims that there might be affectionate, caring relationships between people; but this is to ignore some of the basic features of human life.

For example, we might want to consider the bond between human beings expressed in the mother–child relationship.[15] Sade suggests something of the existential fury that might be read into this relationship; but this is not the only means by which this relationship might be understood. Grace Jantzen has suggested ways in which the emphasis on natality might be explored which do not lead to essentialist formulations of the role of women or the nature of such relationships (Jantzen 1998). In pointing out that all human beings are natals, she provides a possible defence against Sade's claims. Jantzen argues that emphasizing the role that birth plays in defining our humanity reveals the fact that we are all born into human community. We are social beings. At times, we might be born into an inadequate community, but that does not negate the fact that we are formed through a network of relationships. Indeed, once we recognize the significance of relationship for defining our humanity, we are confronted by the need for justice in our dealings with others. Thus, Jantzen is able to develop a sense of the values which can be derived from human experience of this world (in this case, the fundamental reality of relationship), rather than offering an account of such values which sees them as possible only if guaranteed by an other-worldly transcendent (be that 'God' or 'the Good').

The claim that justice can be derived from reflection upon human relationship leads to a further tool with which to combat Sade. Sade's universe is defined by a particular approach to language. It is an approach that furthers the idea of isolation. In Sade's world, only the libertine speaks, the victim is silent; only the libertine acts, the victim is passive. To rework Irigaray's famous comment concerning women (Irigaray 1993: 18): what would it be like if the victim/the other could speak? What if the victim ceased to be a 'victim' and became a 'survivor'? In effect, it is the silence of the victim that allows the libertine to present their ideas as the only possible answer in a world emptied of transcendent value. Even when the victim is allowed to speak, their words are limited and have little force. So Justine's arguments are used as a foil to those of the libertines. In rendering the victim silent, Sade works a sleight of hand. He presents a universe in which his reader is encouraged to identify with the oppressor/libertine. It does not matter what happens to the victim: in their silence they are rendered objects, mere ciphers. This position is maintained by Barthes when he draws attention to the apparent 'irrealism' of Sade's universe:

> Indeed, if some group conceived the desire to realize literally one of the orgies Sade describes . . . the Sadian [sic] scene would quickly be seen to be utterly unreal: the complexity of the combinations, the partners' contortions, the potency of ejaculations, and the victims' endurance all surpass human nature: one would need several arms, several skins, the body of an acrobat, and the ability to achieve orgasm *ad infinitum*. (Barthes 1977: 136)

While Barthes may have a point here, there is a danger that such comments mask the horror of Sade's vision. There is undoubtedly a fantastic dimension to Sade's narrative, but failure to reflect upon the suffering which underpins his libertine's pleasures will simply desensitize the reader to that suffering, perhaps even to suffering more widely understood.

The depersonalization of the victim is a necessary component of Sade's vision, for it enables him to focus entirely upon the libertines. This is where his interest really lies. Consequently, the victims are not drawn as individuals with whom we could identify. Yet if the victim *could* speak, Sade's system would be comprehensively destroyed. While such speech might not force the libertine or the abuser to see the other as a fellow subject, a fellow human being, it would force *the reader* to see the pain.[16] I found reading *120 Days of Sodom* quite unbearable because I could not see the children who are the victims of Sade's libertines as paper children: to me *they were real*. And once that imaginative step has been taken, Sade's world can be seen for the deceit that it is. Sophistry lies behind the libertine's case for his universe. In the words of the victim/survivor, or simply through taking that empathic step, the reader finds a common humanity which is being abused: and it is that mutual recognition that makes the kill or be killed ethic of Sade's universe *wrong*. Human connection challenges the isolated universe of the libertine. This connection can be made through language, but it can also be made through physical contact. The outstretched hand never appears in Sade's writings (Thomas 1995) – hardly surprising, as it is a symbol of connection, trust and intimacy. In order to safeguard ideals of justice, it is not necessary to accept a series of laws ordained by a transcendent God: human contact makes it so.[17]

Defining nature: against 'cruelty' as justification

A further area in which a careful reading of Sade goes some way to negating his conclusions arises from his account of the character of the natural world. Sade's Nature is defined as brutish, unfeeling, callous, violent and destructive. It has to be defined thus in order to provide a justification for the callous, violent and destructive behaviour of Sade's libertines. By acting in the way in which they do, the libertines are simply furthering the ends of nature.

Unqualified talk of 'Nature' is, of course, wrought with difficulties. Our experience of the world around us is always structured by human language and filtered through human categories of thought. In this sense, the habitual distinction made between 'Nature' and 'Culture' is difficult to maintain. It is hard to know what Nature might be *apart from* our apprehension of it. However, it is at least possible to be aware of such difficulties when attempting to describe the 'nature' of Nature. Bearing such qualifications in mind, do the facts of the physical world measure up to Sade's analysis? One of the interesting things about Sade's account of Nature is the way in which he accepts an almost evolutionary account of the natural world. Nature is seen as a self-regulating system that needs both the strong and the weak to maintain its 'perfect equilibrium' (Sade [1791] 1990b: 608). His account of the recycling of matter, which we considered earlier in this chapter in relation to his reflections on death, mirrors recent developments in the way in which the earth's cycles are understood (Lovelock 1995).

It is this implicit understanding of the earth as an integrated ecosystem which goes some way to combating the anthropomorphic presentation of Nature offered by Sade in some parts of his narrative (cf. Sade [1791] 1990b: 608–10). Invariably, Sade uses the persona of 'Mother Nature' to support the brutality of his libertines: yet, in actuality, this Nature is drawn in the likeness of the libertines themselves. Sade suggests that Nature is as gross in its dealings with its creatures as are Sade's libertines with their victims. But this is disingenuous, for Sade uses only those aspects of the natural world that support brutality in drawing his picture of Nature. Even at its most apparently brutal, it is difficult to equate Nature with the acts of Sade's libertines. After all, Nature does not sow up a mother's vagina; Nature does not torture and dismember children. Such acts are born of human volition and will. The natural cycle may include elements that are not friendly to humanity, but this does mean that they are deliberately brutal. Indeed, if we consider those aspects of the natural world that can bring human suffering (for example, volcanoes and earthquakes), we see that these are part of the regulative cycles of the planet. According to geologists, such features may be what makes the world a living and vital place. Without the ever-shifting geological plates on which the continents sit, and the earthquakes and volcanoes which ring them, there would be no recycling of carbon, and consequently no life (Lamb and Sington 1998). From a human perspective, such things may bring suffering, but without these features there would be no human life at all. Justine may have been killed by lightning, but it is not the manner of her death which horrifies the reader: what horrifies is the way in which her corpse is treated *after* her death by Noirceuil and Chabert (Sade [1797] 1968: 1190).[18] In seeking to justify human cruelty, Sade offers an anthropomorphic account of Nature that misrepresents its 'nature'. He seeks to combine the model of human agency with the model of a regulative natural world: and this is simply not analogous. I might have will; Nature does not (or its only will is through mine as I am part of the natural world).

In order to challenge Sade's view of the natural world, then, we do not need to provide alternative features to challenge his sadistic reading. We do not need to proffer a Wordsworthian Nature to balance his Baudelairean vision. Indeed, to trade in contrary examples is to fall into his carefully prepared trap. It is as if we have accepted his anthropomorphic Nature but do not like the way he has drawn 'Her'! If we are to respond effectively to his vision, there has to be the recognition of a major difference between human being and the self-regulating system that is nature.[19] Our humanity is predicated on the fact that we can *choose* how to behave. We are not confined by the laws of nature in the sense that we can set in place value systems; we can create meaning. Nussbaum's comment on the nature of human beings could appropriately be used here:

> No more should we suppose that for a person to live as untutored biological instinct prompts is a better thing, when human beings are deliberating ethical creatures who can control their instincts. (Nussbaum 1994a: 30)

Sade's analysis of nature may be one-sided, in that he never alludes to the beauty of nature and the joy that can be derived from it; but, more importantly, it also supports too narrow and limited an account of the possibilities open to human beings.

Conclusion: towards the meaningful life

Sade challenges any attempt to establish a meaningful sense of human life based upon some kind of transcendent value. However, his account of what constitutes 'transcendence' is, in fact, quite specific. For Sade, the transcendent is understood as that which designates those features of human life that can be distanced from ordinary physical experience. The kind of meaning that he rejects is that which is imposed upon the world from without. It may, however, be possible to retain an idea of 'transcendental value', if this is defined as the value to be derived from the things of this physical world. This seems to me to present a rather different account of what constitutes transcendence. Indeed, even Sade cannot entirely escape from the desire to ascribe a form of transcendence to human being. He might reject any transcendent meaning which is derived from God or reason, but his account of sexuality is clearly predicated upon the possibility that one's desires are open to structure and reflection. Thus he leaves the way open for a transcendental capacity in human being.

However, this form of transcendence does not safeguard notions of human goodness, and, given the violent nature of Sade's universe, this is problematic. Without an ontologically distinct God to support our ethical structures, it might seem that there is no alternative to the violent and bloody account of the universe and human existence that he so graphically presents. Yet analysis of Sade's structure reveals a more complex state of affairs. Sade may have rejected God and reason, but he has retained the dualism that supports these ideas. The place of the all-powerful God has been taken by the libertine, who has the power to create the world after 'his' own image.[20] Reason may have been dethroned, but it is still employed to subjugate the body to the libertine's desires. God and humanity, mind and body, remain distinct entities in his account, and, while he may argue that his philosophy accepts the fundamentally material nature of the universe and humanity, his failure to critique such divisions effectively leads to the injustices attested to in his novels.

Yet a discussion of Sade's ideas can go a long way to aiding the development of a meaningful response to the question of how we should live in this world. For a start, if he rejects mutuality, any ethic grounded in human connection must be a relational one. This relational ethic will not seek to eradicate difference by setting up false dichotomies between master/slave, oppressor/oppressed, libertine/victim. Rather, it will focus on the possibilities of genuine human connection and intimacy for developing an ethic that is grounded in values that can be derived from life in this world.

This in turn will require taking seriously some of the pitfalls that Sade has revealed to us. The significance of sexuality has undoubtedly been ignored by the Western tradition, and feminists, among others, have done much to redress the balance by arguing that this should be placed at the heart of any contemporary spirituality. Sade reveals something of the problems of such a move when it fails to engage with the negative ways in which sexuality can be expressed and exploited. We will need to make a distinction between sexuality understood as sexual acts, and sexuality as it relates to the fact that we are all sexuate beings. To ground one's values simply in sexual expression can lead to a tiresome and monotonous sense of life's meaning: under such an account, my concern lies with where the next fuck is coming from, or how to heighten my sexual responses.

Reading Sade may make us long for the cool reflection of transcendental accounts of the self, and this may involve us taking another step towards the reformulation of that problematic concept 'transcendence'. As we saw in the previous chapter, there may be a way of developing a notion of transcendence as the value to be derived from the things of this world: transcendent value in that sense was not imposed upon us from without, but evolved from human reflection upon physical existence – in that instance, the reflection on the fragility and mutability of a flower. This kind of reflection necessitates a return to the concept of the self: is it possible to accept our fundamental animality while also accepting the reflective possibilities open to us? Can we return to the idea of an 'examined life' without returning to the dualism which distorted previous accounts of mind and body? The dangers of an unreflective life are amply attested to by Justine's stupidity: she is completely unable to reflect upon her existence and the choices that it presents (cf. Sade [1791] 1990b: 693), and thus she lives, not surprisingly, a life of pain and suffering. The aim of the next chapter is to explore the sources that might be available to us for such an enterprise. Can we create a form of meaning in human life which takes seriously the claim that we are embodied beings, but embodied beings with the ability to choose to live in such a way that sex does not distort our personhood, nor death destroy our sense of the joy possible in human life?

5

Living in Accordance with Nature: Seneca

Introduction

For a thesis that seeks to ground an account of the meaningful human life in an acceptance of the fundamental facts of human existence, Sade's universe presents a real challenge. I wish to argue that it is through accepting the basic features of our humanity that we can find a meaningful place in this world: indeed, that 'living in accordance with nature' provides the basis for what this might entail. Such an acceptance may even suggest a different interpretation of what the spiritual life involves than that which relies upon a straightforward polarization of the transcendent and the immanent, and which therefore associates the spiritual with those features of human life that can be distanced from the physical. Sade's challenge lies in his understanding of the implications of an attempt to live in accordance with nature. As we have seen, he suggests that to live thus means to give oneself up to the violent desires of the flesh. Accepting one's grounding in the physical world and one's animal nature necessitates, he argues, a rejection of both contemplation and the possibility of an ethical lifestyle. Sade claims that nature is rapacious and cruel, and that human beings should mirror such features. Somewhat paradoxically, he also argues for an account of sexuality that effectively rejects the 'natural' link between sex and fertility. Indeed, in part his emphasis on anal sex is intended to offer a kind of resistance to the ongoing cycle of reproduction.

But Sade's account is not the only one open to us if we wish to explore what it means to be human. We do not need to juxtapose his account with a conservative rendition of human sexuality that understands human nature as something fixed and unchanging and sexuality only in the context of reproduction. Human life is characterized by its ability to create its own understanding of itself, and it is this creative element which is sometimes forgotten when considering what it means to be sexuate and mortal beings. There is a school of thought, however, that can move us beyond both Sadeian and conservative accounts of human being, and which involves a return to the cradle of Western civilization with which we began this study. Stoicism can be shown to offer an innovative version of what it means to live in accordance with nature. Far from suggesting a brutalizing version of human being, such as that held out by Sade, it offers principles that prove useful for establishing a statement of our humanity that goes beyond any reductionist definition of what this might entail. In arguing for a life lived in accordance with nature, 'nature' is not understood to exclude reason. Thus Stoicism may be able to move us beyond both Sadeian and conservative applications of 'the natural', suggesting ways of rejecting the dualisms of God and nature, sexuality and spirituality, transcendence and immanence. It is for this reason that I wish to end this study with a discussion of the ideas of the Roman philosopher Seneca, whose writings take us beyond such dualisms. Consideration of some of his central beliefs facilitates the development of an account of what it might mean to live in harmony with the universe, locating sexuality and mortality within the contemplative life. The meaningful life is thus that which holds together spirituality and sexuality, transcendence and immanence, reason and reflection. It is the fulfilled and integrated life.

Reclaiming Stoicism and Seneca

In recent years there has been an attempt to reclaim the insights of those schools of philosophy which developed after Plato in Greece, and which continued into the Roman era. Writers such as Margaret Miles, Martha Nussbaum and Pierre Hadot have suggested that what characterizes these schools of thought is the attempt to offer a therapeutic vision of philosophy. Philosophy does not function merely as an academic exercise, but provides a way of solving the problems posed by living in this world. In this sense, the philosopher is conceived as physician (Nussbaum 1994a: 3). By exploring this analogy, those seeking to reclaim the ideas of these Hellenistic schools argue that we must move beyond (and behind) the assumptions of countless commentators who have viewed the ideas of such philosophers through the filter of post-Enlightenment understandings of philosophy (Miles 1999: 169). We are dealing not simply with academic game-play but with a vision of a philosophy that offers a guide for living.[1]

It is this practical focus that shall be pursued here. The decision to concentrate upon a Stoic philosopher arises from a variety of reasons. In contrast to some figures in the history of Western philosophy,[2] the Stoic school lent itself to a positive valuation of women: there is no reason why a woman should be excluded from a Stoic lifestyle and, moreover, no reason why women should not practise philosophy.[3] Indeed, Seneca tells his mother, Helvia, to commit herself to study as a way of overcoming her sorrow at his exile (Seneca 1997b: 24).[4] In part, such a conclusion rests upon the denial of the kind of dualism which has distinguished mind from matter, soul from body, and which has been so damaging for women, who have been associated with the subordinate member of these binary oppositions (cf. B. Clack 1999: 1–9). Instead, an understanding of human being is offered which defines reason as crucial to our humanity, yet does not seek to distance it from the physical experience of being human. In particular, human mortality is accepted in a way that does not render human life meaningless: it is this acceptance that will form the focus for our discussion.

It might still be felt that the work of Lucius Annaeus Seneca (*c.*4BCE–65CE) provides a rather strange starting point for a contemporary discussion of the meaningful life. Seneca has been accorded a somewhat dubious place in the history of philosophy. He was tutor to the emperor Nero, and the description of him as the 'tyrant's tutor' has stuck (Griffin [1976] 1992: 148). F. H. Sandbach, one of his fiercest critics, accuses him of 'flattery and falsehood' (Sandbach [1989] 1994: 153) in his dealings with the young emperor, characterized, he claims, by the tone of the essay 'On mercy' (Seneca 1995b), a piece addressed to Nero. Alongside this political miring, Seneca is invariably castigated as the philosopher who emphasized the simple life, romanticizing poverty, while himself being exceedingly rich.[5] The charge of hypocrisy is frequently made: according to Robin Campbell, he is 'history's most notable example of a man who failed to live up to his principles' (Seneca 1969: 14). Such character assassination is common: Sandbach calls him 'insincere and a windbag' (Sandbach [1989] 1994: 162).

Yet despite such comments, women in particular seem to find something appealing about his ideas.[6] Perhaps this is because women, more than men, are used to working out of what Gillian Rose calls 'the broken middle' (Rose 1992), working with what is, rather than with what ought to be. If anything, a certain respect can arise for a man who tried to counsel Nero in the ways of clemency; rather than reading this work as hypocrisy and flattery, it is possible to view it as an attempt to impress upon an unstable and dissolute man the need for just rule. It is perhaps this willingness to grapple with the situated nature of his works that differentiates his critics from his admirers. Sandbach draws attention to the inconsistencies in Seneca's work (Sandbach [1989] 1994: 159), but it may be in precisely this that his relevance is to be found. After all, life is full of inconsistencies and ambiguities. Sandbach's comments resonate with scholastic prejudices that fail to take seriously either Seneca's context or the form his writing takes.[7] Pierre Hadot's work has emphasized the significance of the form in which different philosophies are written: in the case of Hellenistic philosophy, he claims that these texts are written as spiritual exercises (Hadot [1987] 1995: 52). Thus it can be argued that Seneca's writings are less a set of systematized writings, and more a set of specific responses to specific questions and problems. In this sense, applying the philosophical criteria of consistency is both inappropriate to the form and irrelevant to the content.

This is not to say that one should not be suspicious of a rich man who exalts the simple life.[8] Yet his wealth was not to protect him from the transiency of human life: his son died in infancy (Griffin [1976] 1992: 57–8). Similarly, the way in which he approached his death somewhat undermines the charge of hypocrisy. He was ordered to commit suicide by Nero, and Tacitus gives a powerful account of the way in which he did this which seems wholly consistent with the Stoic principles he espoused (cf. Tacitus 1977: 375–7).

In considering Seneca's ideas I am deliberately emphasizing those elements of his thought that support the construction of an integrated account of human being that takes seriously embodiment and which resists a solution to the problem of death based exclusively upon notions of transcendent value or a transcendent horizon. This selective view is not, I think, problematic; if anything, it applies a criterion to his thought of which Seneca would have approved. Stoicism encourages flexibility in the use of source material: so, as we shall see, Seneca was not averse to using Epicurean ideas if they suited his arguments. Such a methodology may explain why Stoicism has been one of the most adaptable and long-lived of the Hellenistic schools. Recent interpretations are to be found in both Nietzsche[9] and Wittgenstein,[10] and it is my contention that some of these ideas might be used as the basis for an account of the meaningful life (or even a spirituality) peculiarly suited to the twenty-first century.

Spirituality, religion and God

When spirituality is discussed, there is an understandable tendency to equate it with religion. The word itself suggests a concern with the 'spirit', which seems to imply an interest in the pre-eminent spirit itself, God. This can lead to the idea that any discussion of 'the spiritual life' must involve a religious dimension. 'Religion' apparently refers to a range of experiences – not only to personal religious experience, but also to institutional and ritualistic responses to life (Clack and Clack 1998: 1–5). Associated with this definition is the idea that meaning is to be found elsewhere: with gods or God, with a higher reality, with something that transcends the human. Yet spirituality need not be defined thus: it is possible to offer a broader definition for what constitutes 'the spiritual life'. For example, Margaret Miles suggests that the neo-Platonist Plotinus offers a 'secular theology' (Miles 1999: 178), which she describes, in terms borrowed from Charles Winquist, as 'a thinking within the ordinariness of experience that makes a difference within the ordinariness of experience' (quoted in Miles 1999: 178). Religion and spirituality need not be understood symbiotically. Indeed, an antipathy to all things religious is found in the Hellenistic schools. The Stoics often resist the idea that the patterns of life laid out by the 'religious' are appropriate when it comes to determining the character of the meaningful life.[11] Spirituality becomes, instead, an entire response to being in this world (cf. Miles 1999: 15) – a response which is connected not simply with those features of life that might be categorized as of the soul or the inner life. So, in Pierre Hadot's analysis of ancient philosophy as a way of life, he discerns an account of the spiritual life that requires practical effort and training, a life that involves 'the entire spirit, *one's whole way of being*' (Hadot [1987] 1995: 21; my emphasis). This goes some way to explaining the nature of these philosophers' writings: in pointing out that they are to be understood as spiritual exercises, Hadot draws attention to the way in which such writings are intended to support growth and maturity. These writings are not theoretical exercises but practical responses to the situations faced on a daily basis. For example, some spiritual exercises offer imaginative engagements with poverty, suffering and death, and are designed to create habits in our thinking and being which stand up to the onslaught from such factors or events (cf. Hadot [1987] 1995: 85). The philosopher is not a philosopher, then, because of what he or she *knows*, but 'because of his existential attitude' ([1987] 1995: 30). Similarly, according to Nussbaum's reflections on ancient philosophy, spirituality does not arise from a desire to evade the realities of life, but involves an engagement *with* life, finding in its very mundanity the profundity possible in mutable human existence.[12]

The dismissive attitude towards popular religion reflects a similar ambivalence towards the idea of God. God is defined interchangeably as 'Nature', or 'Providence', or as the rational centre of the universe. Commentators such as Sandbach might assume a traditional theistic definition when the word 'God' appears in Stoic writings, but this seems to gloss the complex nature of the Stoic God. The identification of God/Nature/Providence necessitates a more open interpretation of the character of this word. Ultimately it does not matter what (or who) created this world: what matters is that the fundamental feature of human being – rationality – means that we have the opportunity to share in the rational character of this universe. And this stands whatever happens to lie behind the existence of this universe. So Seneca can write: 'whether we have been allotted to a god's protection or abandoned to the whim of fortune . . .' (Seneca 1997a: 100), while never suggesting that one's interpretation of existence will necessitate a choice between different sets of values. In practice, it seems that the belief in God/gods is irrelevant. What matters is that we live well, and that philosophy provides us with a guide for living the good life:

> Whether we are caught in the grasp of an inexorable law of fate, whether it is God who as lord of the universe has ordered all things, or whether the affairs of mankind are tossed and buffeted haphazardly by chance, it is philosophy that has the duty of protecting us. (Letter XVI; Seneca 1969: 64)

A similar point is made when Seneca notes that life might be the gift of the gods, but living *well* is the gift of philosophy (Letter XC; 1969: 161). This seems to suggest that belief in God/gods has little to do with the issue of *how* one is to live. In this sense, the Stoic approach to life is equally relevant for theist or non-theist.[13]

At times, however, a stronger commitment to God is expressed. Then, God is described as 'our teacher' (Seneca 1995d: 278), a depiction suggestive of a more thorough-going theism. Yet even in this context, a subtly different account of the divine emerges than that which characterizes philosophical theism.[14] For Seneca, 'God' is simply another name for 'nature': 'For what is nature if not god and divine reason pervading the entire world and its parts?' (Seneca 1995d: 278). This suggests something of the pantheistic flavour of Stoicism, and, as we shall see, it has considerable ramifications for the way in which reason is understood. Indeed, such a definition suggests that the injunction to live in accordance with nature will have quite different ramifications from those suggested by Sade's philosophy.

Nature and the goal of human life

Aristotle argued that the goal of human life was *eudaimonia*, usually translated as 'happiness', but more accurately rendered as 'contentment' or 'fulfilment'. The philosophical schools that followed him made it their business to provide frameworks for living which realized this goal. For the Stoic, achieving *eudaimonia* was simple: to be truly happy, one must live in accordance with nature (Seneca, Letter V; 1969: 37). The simplicity of this solution is illustrated by an example Seneca gives: a child is born with all that it needs for a fulfilling human life.[15] The child does not base the meaning of its existence upon the things that surround it (Seneca 1997b: 6). It has within itself that which can make it happy. That which lies outside the self is of little importance; the only true happiness is to be found in self-reliance, and this is located at the beginning of human life.

Of course, the simplicity of this solution is a little deceptive. The term 'nature' is notoriously difficult to define. Sandbach has highlighted the ambiguity of the Stoic definition. At times, 'nature' seems to refer to a material force 'constituent of the body it controls' (Sandbach [1989] 1994: 31); in other words, that which is 'normal' for a particular species. At other times, it seems to have a broader meaning, referring to that which governs the world – a living being 'identical with God' (Sandbach [1989] 1994: 32). Indeed, sometimes Seneca follows this pattern, defining nature in terms analogous to God or Providence. At others, he uses this term to imply the universe. At the very least there seems to be an interchangeability of meaning which defies the usual distinctions made between the divine and the world. This fits well with the Stoic perception of the universe: there is no dualistic under-standing of nature and the divine. The universe is one; all that is, is physical, and this means that human beings are not radically distinct from the physical universe, but are an integral part of the universe itself.

Even moving beyond the problems posed by this definition of na-ture, there remains the question of the *quality* of the life that is to be lived in accordance with it. Seneca provides a powerful interpretation of what he understands such a life to involve:

> I live according to Nature if I devote myself wholly to her, if I marvel at her and worship her. Nature wished me to do both – to act and to be free for contemplation. I am doing both. Even contemplation involves action. (Seneca 1995c: 177).

This emphasis on the contemplation of nature suggests something of the significance of Seneca's thought. Dualistic accounts of reason and nature, mind and body, that have shaped Western philosophical de-bates have tended to emphasize the opposition between these features; so much so, that it can come as something of a surprise when one finds an explanation that seeks to dispel such dualisms. In practice, Seneca is not alone in offering such an account of reason; Plotinus, for exam-ple, pictures the universe as a 'single mighty living thing' (*Ennead*, 4.4.11–12; Miles 1999: 77), a vision that undercuts any dualistic dis-tinction between mind and body. In defining reason thus, Seneca is simply following the precepts of his school. For Seneca, as for earlier Stoics, reason is not understood as that which transcends the body and the physical universe: rather, it is that which characterizes the *natural* human life. The reasoned life is *nature's* intention for human beings. As Nussbaum puts it, for the Stoics, reasoning is 'our piece of the divinity which inhabits the whole framework of the universe' (Nussbaum 1994a: 326). If we are to live in accordance with nature, we must realize our contemplative selves. Such thinking leads to a high view of philosophy, for it is only the pursuit of wisdom that makes one fully alive (Seneca 1997d: 75). Indeed, Seneca goes so far as to say that the happy life is impossible without the pursuit of wisdom (Letter XVI; 1969: 63).

The integrated vision of nature and reason finds a ready resonance with the work of present-day feminist philosophers, such as Susan Griffin, who argue that the mind itself is physical (cf. Griffin 1989: 103). Similarly, when Seneca argues that 'man is a rational animal' (Letter XLI; 1969: 88), this definition depends upon a broader under-standing of reason than simply that which associates it with the mind and which distances it from the body. Mind *and* body are part of the integrated human life. As Nussbaum puts it, 'reasoning does not sim-ply produce intellectual conviction, it changes the life of desire' (in Ward 1996: 205). In this sense, the process of self-scrutiny is inti-mately connected with the therapeutic process of self-realization. Re-flection upon the self, as with Freudian analysis, leads to a change in perspective that similarly affects the way in which one acts.[16]

The integration of mind and body is clarified by considering the complexity of the Stoic account of the passions. Here, in contrast to Platonic thought, the passions are understood cognitively. They are not features to be distinguished from the rational faculty. In other words, the passions arise out of our rational nature. They are socially constructed, rather than pre-rational, and this means that they can be manipulated. Passions such as anger or grief occur when reason is impaired or improperly used; yet this means that they can be changed and controlled.

Understanding the rational formation of the passions goes some way to explaining that which to contemporary eyes may seem to be the strangest aspect of Stoic thought: if one is to live the life of a wise 'man', to live in accordance with nature, one must 'extirpate' the pas-sions. Some examples may prove useful here. We might think of emo-tions as fundamental to our humanity; and the Stoic need not disagree at this point. Emotion is not the problem: *passions* are. Passions sig-nify a loss of self-control at odds with the life lived according to rea-son. So, for example, Seneca seeks to show why anger should be eradicated from the life of the philosopher (Seneca 1995a). We might think anger against injustice is a good thing, but Seneca disagrees: far from showing us to be caring humans, it turns us into the image of that to which we are responding in the first place (cf. Nussbaum 1994a: 422). Anger – even that which is righteous – is brutalizing. Rather than react angrily to injustice, Seneca emphasizes the importance of self-reflection and self-criticism. We must remember that we are not perfect. Yet there is a tension in Seneca's thought here: when confronted by stories that reflect the tyranny of rulers, Seneca himself seems to display anger at injustice and cruelty (Nussbaum 1994a: 434–5). This would seem to suggest that the extirpation of anger would involve the extirpation of something that is an appropriate human response.

The main reason for rejecting the passions lies in the sense that they lead us to misconstrue our relationship to the universe as a whole. Reason, properly used, allows us to place our lives within the overall pattern of the natural world. We come to see things from nature's perspective, and this has a radical impact on what we consider to be 'good' and 'evil'. As Hadot puts it, 'we are to switch from our "human" vision of reality, in which our values depend on our passions, to a "natural" vision of things, which replaces each event within the perspective of universal nature' (Hadot [1987] 1995: 83). Part of the problem, the Stoic argues, is that we invariably attach terms such as 'good' and 'evil' to the things that happen around us and to us. Yet if we could see things from nature's point of view we would value these occurrences somewhat differently. A volcano, for example, should not be considered 'evil', as it is simply acting according to the needs of the universe. As Marcus Aurelius notes, change, transience and death are necessary in order that 'different things may come to be' (XII: 21; Aurelius 1998: 114). Similarly, it is pointless to bewail the inevitability of one's death: 'You will go the way that all things go. What is strange about that?' (Letter LXXVII: Seneca 1969: 128). Death is not evil: it is simply part of the nature of the universe. The emphasis on the contemplative life has, then, a practical import: it enables the acceptance of the transience that characterizes human life. At the heart of such an acceptance lies the radical decentring of the human person:

> We are not the world's reason for bringing back winter and summer. These follow laws of their own, which govern things divine. We think too well of ourselves, if we see ourselves as the worthy objects of such mighty motions. None of them is there to wrong us. Indeed, none occurs except to our benefit. (Seneca 1995a: 64)

These words are rather shocking when read for the first time, immured as we are in a culture which assumes that the seasons have been introduced for our benefit, or at least are open to human manipulation and control. Stoicism necessitates a comprehensive revisioning of humanity's place within the overall structure of the universe. This is a difficult transformation, and the purpose of the spiritual exercise is to facilitate this change (cf. Hadot [1987]1995: 83). Displacing our selves and our experiences from the centre of the universe involves practice and commitment. We must learn that the things that happen to us are not so important. This suggests, as Nussbaum has indicated, a tension between personal tragedy and the requirements of the whole (Nussbaum 1994a: 223). Yet focusing on what might be called 'the bigger picture' does not mean that human life is reduced to a mechanistic and materialistic experience. If good and evil cannot be assigned to the externals of our existence, they are terms applicable to the evaluation of our own actions. Reason becomes even more important, for it provides the tool with which to decide the limits of our responsibility.

This sense of personal responsibility goes some way to explaining the Stoic attitude to both slaves and women. I might not be able to change the world around me, but I can control my responses to it, and this is true for all human beings, regardless of their social status. Thus, the wise man is not simply located in the leisured classes, as is the case with, say, Aristotle: there is no reason why a slave or a woman should not similarly achieve the goal of human life. Initially, this sounds positively egalitarian. Yet there seems little awareness of the extent to which one's social placing will impact upon one's ability to live the life of the philosopher. The fact that the private sphere is a possible realm for philosophical activity ignores the differences in status between being a woman (of that time) or a slave, and being a retired, wealthy man. For either of the former, the domestic sphere is a place of work; for the last it is a place of relaxation that is itself dependent upon the work of the other two. As Janet Martin Soskice has indicated, it is far from clear that the traditional formulations of what constitutes the spiritual/philosophical life can easily be undertaken by women engaged in the traditional roles of child-rearing and house-keeping (Soskice 1992). Stoicism does little to challenge such unjust social structures.[17] A contemporary spirituality need not accept these conclusions. And, indeed, if we are seeking to break down the dualistic forms of philosophical thinking, we will want to unite thought and action in ways that reflect the attempt to bring together the properties traditionally ascribed to the transcendent and the immanent. Inner transformation and social change could be understood as just as connected as reason and nature, mind and body. Indeed, the methodology Seneca promotes seems to suggest such an end. He is at pains to tell others to use their own resources, rather than simply accepting his ideas (Letter XXXIII; 1969: 80). The patient is to become her own physician (Nussbaum 1994a: 317). Dependence upon the teacher is not encouraged, which highlights a major difference between the Stoics and their rivals, the Epicureans, who accorded Epicurus the status of a god (cf. Nussbaum 1994a: 130). Seneca, by way of contrast, promotes a maturity that suggests that human nature itself is trustworthy: it has not been warped by any metaphysical concept such as 'sin'. Whether we become good or bad people is up to us and the kind of lives we decide to create.

An awareness of what one can and cannot control is vital to the ethical code Seneca promotes. To live in accordance with nature, one must loosen the hold of fortune. Fortune, fate or chance (*Tyche*) was divinized by many Romans as the Goddess Fortuna (cf. Turcan [1992] 1996) – hardly surprising in a culture acutely aware of the mutability of human existence. The Stoic response is to argue that, if we are to be happy, we must live in such a way that what happens to us does not affect us. Much of human life is characterized by transience: that which gives our life meaning can all too easily be taken away by circumstance, another, or even death itself. Seneca's solution is to argue that we must not regard as valuable 'anything that is capable of being taken away' (Letter IX; 1969: 52). In other words, living the life of the wise man involves refusing to provide any hostages to fortune.

Seneca's response seems particularly cold at this point. He seems to be saying that we should avoid too deep a connection with other human beings in case they are taken from us, leaving us bereft of their presence – a claim which resonates with Augustine's response to the losses that he endured. As we shall see, there is a similar tension in Seneca's thought to that discerned in Augustine's theology. Like Augustine, Seneca places a high value upon relationship, and particularly friendship. For now, let us follow his argument through. To combat the blows of fortune, we must train ourselves to see human life from nature's point of view. At the same time, we must recognize that which is within our control – that is, our *response* to the things that happen to us. In this setting, the extirpation of the passions becomes less a peculiar quirk and more a necessity. The passions effectively place us in Fortune's hands: anger assumes things should not have gone as they have, that there is a kind of control open to us; pity, that things should not have gone as they have for another; and so on. By giving into the passions, we give into wrong thinking, and thus capitulate to Fortune.

Seneca's ethic is not, however, inhuman. He is at pains to recognize both the strength of the passions and the appropriateness of certain forms of emotion. His *Consolation* to his mother Helvia, written during his exile, recognizes the difficulty of combating grief: 'no strong feeling is under our control, least of all that which arises from sorrow' (Seneca 1997b: 23). A distinction needs to be made between emotion – perfectly natural human responses – and the passions – characterized as 'mental disturbances'. So Marcus Aurelius writes of the need to be 'entirely passionless and yet full of natural affection' (*Meditations*, 1: 9; Aurelius 1998: 4). Love of children and friends is thus good and proper: problems arise only when one accords a status to these relationships that they do not have. To base the meaning of our lives on such relationships will mean that we deliver ourselves into Fortune's hands, as these things are subject to decay and death. (Of course, we need to ask if it is really so simple to distinguish between emotion and passion in this way, or, indeed, if life lived with such a mitigated sense of the importance of others would really be worth living.)

If we follow Seneca's advice and seek to see things from nature's point of view, we can resist delivering ourselves into Fortune's fickle hands by living firmly in the present. This may be of particular help for modern people, 'hypnotized as we are by language, images, information, and the myth of the future' (Hadot [1987] 1995: 235). Resisting the pull of both past and present, we can overcome the perils of both hope and fear (Letter V; Seneca 1969: 38). As Seneca puts it: 'Never have I trusted Fortune, even when she seemed to offer peace' (Seneca 1997b: 6). Seneca offers a practical outlook that can shape our response to the things that happen to us in this world. Living according to nature involves adopting what could be called a transcendent viewpoint – what Hadot describes as a 'cosmic consciousness' ([1987] 1995: 85) – aligning oneself imaginatively with the cycles of the natural world, putting one's life into the wider perspective of the universe. But this form of transcendence does not mean that we should deny the transiency of human life, or that we should see ourselves as capable of transcending/escaping the physical universe. Indeed, the most fertile ground for an understanding of how we should live in this world comes through a contemplation of death that takes seriously the reality and implications of human mortality.

Death and immortality

> Well, then, have you just now realized that death looms over you, or
> exile, or anguish? You were born to these things. Let us reflect that
> whatever can happen is going to happen. (Letter XXIV; Seneca 1997a:
> 90)

According to Seneca, the human condition is defined by death and
trouble. Far from being aberrations, these are fundamental features of
human existence. We should not, then, be surprised when misfortune
befalls us. But, along with his rejection of externals as either good or
bad, Seneca focuses on that which is in our control: our *responses* to
such occurrences. In this sense, he is concerned with the ethical response to death. The fear of death leads to all kinds of bad actions:
greed, betrayal, cowardice. As Seneca puts it: 'He will live badly who
does not know how to die well' (Seneca 1997c: 48).

In order to support the formation of the good life, Seneca provides
examples designed to conquer the fear of death. This is vital for culti-
vating the tranquillity of the good life, for he contends that, once the
fear of death is conquered, nothing remains to be feared (Letter XXIV;
1997a: 89). Adopting an argument framed by Epicurus, fear of death
is conquered once it is shown that death is simply 'not-being'. Moreover, we should not fear this as constituting an alien experience, for
we have already experienced what this is like:

> Death is just not being. What that is like I know already. It will be the
> same after me as it was before me. If there is any torment in the later
> state, there must also have been torment in the period before we saw the
> light of day; yet we never felt conscious of any distress then. I ask you,
> wouldn't you say that anyone who took the view that a lamp was worse
> off when it was put out than it was before it was lit was an utter idiot?
> We, too, are put out. We suffer somewhat in the intervening period, but
> at either end of it there is a deep tranquillity. (Letter LIV; 1969: 104–5)

The ease with which Seneca dispels the fear of death can, of course,
be challenged. Yet while commentators such as Nussbaum are critical
of his claim that the fear of death could be so easily dissolved, adopting Hadot's reading of such passages as spiritual exercises may go
some way to forming a more positive response. Hadot in effect suggests that what we have in such passages – and in similar passages

offered by Lucretius and Marcus Aurelius – is a form of cognitive therapy. This is an exercise to train the mind, and, in that sense, is offered as a way of coming to terms with one's impending death.

Seneca's thought reflects the agnosticism of Stoicism more generally when he considers precisely what happens after death. The soul/life (*psyche*) of the self is understood to be material, and therefore is not believed to survive the body's dissolution. In common with other Stoics, Seneca focuses on the return of the human self to the stuff of the universe. With death, the human self is dispersed, returned to, and reunited with the fundamental elements of the universe.[18] As such, the ideal death is characterized as the 'gentle process of dissolution' (Letter XXVI; 1969: 70–71) that comes about through the process of ageing. Thus there is an acceptance of the cycle of birth, decay, death and reconstitution at the heart of Seneca's thinking which mirrors the grounding of one's life in the processes of the universe.

Preparing for one's death becomes part of the practice of life (cf. Seneca 1997d: 66). Like Plato, Seneca seems to accept the idea that the philosophical life will be characterized by the discipline of 'practising death'. However, while Plato relates this practice to the denial of the flesh in favour of the mind, Seneca interprets it rather differently: in reflecting upon death, we take life and its limited time-span seriously (cf. Seneca 1997d: 59–83). Indeed, the emphasis placed on the inevitability of death arises from Seneca's concern to convince his reader of the limited time available to each human life. Once we become aware of this, we will use our time wisely. We will ensure that 'we do not waste our energies pointlessly or in pointless activities' (1997d: 50). To live thus means an end to the complaint that life is too short: 'It is not that we have a short time to live, but that we waste a lot of it' (1997d: 59).

The theme of living in the present is closely connected to this point: 'Live immediately' (1997d: 68). If you live like this, there is plenty of time: it is only the wastefulness of one's time that makes life short. Such an approach challenges existentialist accounts of the tension between past, present and future as that which characterizes human life. Similarly, it suggests something of the problem with contemporary living, where much faith is placed in the future through insurance, pensions and career plans. To make every moment worth while means that, when death comes, it will be met 'with a firm step' (1997d: 71). Indeed, one's deathbed is viewed as an event that reveals how well one has lived (Letter XXVI; 1969: 71). One can even anticipate what this will be like during life, rehearsing one's death as a way of assessing the meaning of one's life:

> Without anxiety, then, I'm making ready for the day when the tricks and disguises will be put away and I shall come to a verdict on myself, determining whether the courageous attitudes I adopt are really felt or just so many words . . . Away with the world's opinion of you – it's always unsettled and divided. Away with the pursuits that have occupied the whole of your life – death is going to deliver the verdict in your case. . . . It's only when you're breathing your last that the way you've spent your life will become apparent. I accept the terms, and feel no dread of the coming judgement. (Letter XXVI; 1969: 71)

The meaning of death is thus located in life, and this position leads to a highly critical view of the belief in immortality. Seneca is concerned that the illusion of an immortal existence might lead to time being wasted in this life:

> You are living as if destined to live for ever; your own frailty never occurs to you; you don't notice how much time has already passed, but squander it as though you had a full and overflowing supply – though all the while that very day which you are devoting to somebody or something may be your last. You act like mortals in all that you fear, and like immortals in all that you desire. (1997d: 62)

While Seneca is undoubtedly referring to the lack of thought given to the inevitability of death, this comment suggests something of the ambivalence felt towards the concept of immortality itself in Stoic thought. There is a vagueness towards it in Marcus Aurelius,[19] and what Miriam Griffin calls an agnosticism in Seneca's own thought (Griffin [1976] 1992: 175). When he addresses the question of the soul's immortality, he does not provide a firm answer, preferring to focus on what *might* be the case: '*if it survives the body*, it can in no way be destroyed, since no sort of immortality is qualified and nothing can damage what is eternal' (Letter LVII; Seneca 1997a: 94; my emphasis). Similarly, he is comfortable with whatever might transpire: 'If we are released, the better part of us remains having lost its burden; if we are destroyed, nothing remains and good and evil alike are removed' (Letter XXIV; Seneca 1997a: 91). Indeed, Seneca seems to suggest that whether or not there is an immortal dimension to human existence is irrelevant to the question of how one should live: he never suggests that the lack of an immortal existence would render the good life a waste of time. Where he does refer more positively to the concept of immortality, he tends to link it to the mind's ability to transcend one's physical place through study (and in this sense follows Aristotle), rather than simply interpreting it as 'surviving death'. Thus the philosopher 'is not confined by the same boundary as are others. He alone is free from the laws that limit the human race, and all ages serve him as though he were a god' (Seneca 1997d: 77–8). Rather than a dogmatic belief in the immortality of the soul, what appears to matter more is that the transience of life should be accepted (Letter XCI; 1969: 179): it is, after all, part of the natural order of things. The wise man will not berate his lot, but accept that these are the terms for his existence:

> There's no ground for resentment in all this. We've entered into a world in which these are the terms life is lived on – if you're satisfied with that, submit to them, if you're not, get out, whatever way you please. (Letter XCI; 1969: 181–2)[20]

Death is part of the natural order of things, and it is ridiculous not to accept that this is the case: 'No one in his right mind is angry with nature' (Seneca 1995a: 50).

Further analysis of Seneca's ideas on death can undercut criticisms that might be made of his concern with mortality. His preoccupation with death could leave him open to the charge that he is espousing a 'necrophilic' (Jantzen 1998) or death-loving philosophy, or that his work displays a 'morbid asceticism' (Griffin [1976] 1992: 177). Yet both characterizations miss the significance of the connection between life and death that he makes. He might argue for a correlation between the extent to which we fear death and the significance we give to life (Letter XXVI; 1969: 72); but at the same time he does not argue that we should cease to love mutable human existence: 'the man . . . you should admire and imitate is the one who finds it a joy to live and inspite of that is not reluctant to die' (Letter LV; 1969: 105).

Undoubtedly there is a complex account of death offered in Seneca's writings. At times he does seem to downplay the business of living by focusing upon the manner in which one should approach one's actual death (cf. Letter LXXVII; 1969: 126). Yet Hadot's discussion of Marcus Aurelius' exercises on death may go some way to clarifying how this complexity should be understood. Hadot argues that when Marcus Aurelius describes the putridity of matter he is not passing a judgement on the body, but rather showing us that what seems repugnant is, in reality, part of the natural processes of the cosmos (Hadot [1987] 1995: 188; reflection on Aurelius IX, 1998: 36). A similar process is at work in Seneca's writings. Indeed, it is a misrepresentation to say that he is obsessed with suicide and glorifies death. In one of his letters to Lucilius, he rejects outright any irrational desire to end one's life. Such a 'passion for dying' (Letter XXIV; 1997a: 92) should be resisted: if one does take one's own life it should not be because the passions have excited one to the act. Rather, it should occur after one has made a reasoned response to the facts of one's existence – if, in the circumstances, it is the best thing to do.

Moreover, the idea that one can juxtapose mortality with the paradigm of natality is sharply refuted in Seneca's work. He is concerned with death and how one might approach it: but alongside such reflections, designed to aid the business of living, he also offers natality as the basis for the egalitarianism of Stoic ethics. 'All of us', he writes, 'have the same beginnings, the same origin.' He goes on: 'We all have one common parent – the cosmos' (Seneca 1995d: 262). Life and death, natality and mortality, are part of the whole that is human life. Reflection on death results in a fuller comprehension of what it means to live in accordance with nature. It is an attitude that leads us to grasp the interconnection and symmetry of these aspects of the whole that is human life.

The individual in relationship

This emphasis on the interconnection between all things leads to an aspect of Seneca's thought which might seem out of step with some of the stereotypical ideas of what Stoicism involves: relationship and friendship. The individual provides the starting point for the Stoic response to the world. The use of reason and the importance given to self-sufficiency are key tenets of Stoic thought; yet Seneca also emphasizes the importance of relationship. The individual is always an individual in community.[21] Hadot suggests that such an understanding derives from reflection upon human life as part of the whole that is the universe: in such a context, we cannot understand ourselves as 'alone' (Hadot [1987] 1995: 34). The individual can be understood only in relation to others. Indeed, Seneca is at pains to emphasize the importance of family ties: there is a joy to be found in children and grandchildren (Seneca 1997b: 25). While Seneca recognizes this, and indeed counsels his mother to experience this joy as a counterbalance to her sorrow at his exile, he is also at pains to identify the fundamentally fragile happiness to be found in such relationships. It is always possible that one's loved ones will be removed from this life by death. Here the tension in Stoic thought arises: in seeking tranquillity, there is a tendency to focus upon that which cannot be destroyed. At the same time, the down-to-earth nature of Stoic ethics necessitates the acceptance of familial relationships as important. Can we accept both the joy of our relationships and the potential sorrow that comes from grounding life's meaning in such mutable beings? Nussbaum suggests that for the Stoic the extirpation of the passions is the answer: 'The world's vulnerable gifts, cherished, give rise to the passionate life; despised, to a life of calm' (Nussbaum 1994a: 389).

There is some evidence for Nussbaum's claim. At times, Seneca seems to advocate that one should affect a mindset that places a distance between oneself and loved ones, recognizing that death is an ever-present possibility. Wisdom comes from accepting this state of affairs with equanimity (Seneca 1997c: 48–9). Yet there are other features of his thought that suggest that things are not so clear-cut as Nussbaum would have it. As well as recognizing the pain that comes from making oneself vulnerable to the other, Seneca argues that this recognition does not undermine their worth: rather their company should be enjoyed in the here and now, finding in each moment the precious quality of that connection (cf. Seneca 1969: 115; Letter LXIII).

When considered with Seneca's writing on friendship, such comments further undercut a simplistic reading of where true tranquillity might lie. Letter XLVIII begins with a statement exalting the importance of friendship. Elsewhere, friendship is placed alongside reason as the gift of the gods to 'men': 'God has given that vulnerable creature ['man'] two things that make him strongest of all, reason and fellowship' (Seneca 1995d: 288). Such passages suggest a different picture of Stoicism from the caricature of the lone individual standing out against death and the world. Indeed, the vital importance of human communication is recognized. Conversation with friends is the key method for attaining truth (cf. Nussbaum 1994a: 377), a view that draws upon the long history of the dialogue as a tool for philosophical training. Yet such conversation need not be understood as dry and academic: laughter and leisure are also deemed important, and even drunkenness, on occasion, is no bad thing (Seneca 1997c:

58). As Seneca puts it, 'laughter, and a lot of it, is the right response to the things which drive us to tears' (Seneca 1995a: 108).

Two points can be drawn from this: firstly, despite comments to the contrary, it would seem that the acceptance of transient life informing Nussbaum's own ideas *is* acknowledged in Seneca's world. The apparently contradictory features that make up his view of the universe and the individual lead Nussbaum to the conclusion that Seneca is 'deeply committed both to Stoicism and to the world, both to purity and to the erotic' (Nussbaum 1994a: 471). Perhaps such comments should be understood not as contradictions, but simply as evidence of an appropriately well-rounded attitude to the world. Life is varied: it does consist of joy and sorrow, hope and despair, fulfilment and tragedy, and what one gets from an engagement with Seneca is a sense of the connection between these apparently polarized features.

Secondly, in relation to the general argument of this book, the Stoic account of the individual in relation goes some way to providing tools for a rejection of Sade's account of what it means to live in accordance with nature. In Seneca's Stoicism one finds an account of humanity that denies that the 'natural' human existence is defined by a desire to kill, fuck and maim. Rather, relationship and laughter stand alongside reason in the Stoic narrative of human being. When one reads Seneca, one gets the impression that what is being offered is a picture of human life which reflects the real and complex business of being human.

Conclusion: beyond Stoicism

In this chapter I have suggested areas of Seneca's thought which might be used to develop a contemporary account of the meaningful human life that takes seriously its grounding in the life of the universe. However, it would be a mistake to suggest that all aspects of his thought, and indeed of Stoicism more generally, can be understood as friendly to the kind of approach to human meaning I am attempting to formulate.

For a start, in places Seneca seems to question the extent to which bodily existence can be understood positively, and this raises questions about the possibility of grounding the meaningful human life in an acceptance of the primacy of human embodiment. At times, Seneca suggests that the body is a burden (Letter LXV; 1969: 122). At others, he appears to question the engagement with physical existence: 'Petty is the mind which delights in earthly things' (1997b: 12) (although this comment probably refers less to the material universe and more to the shallowness and superficiality of many human concerns). In similar vein, he seems to offer at points a problematization of sexuality that paves the way for asceticism. Pleasure is resisted, while procreation is seen as the only justifiable reason for sexual intercourse (1997b: 19).

Yet perhaps an awareness of the ambiguity of physical existence is no bad thing. After all, living with a healthy body may be a joy, living with a sick or dying one, less so. Similarly, Margaret Miles locates such comments in the contemporary context of Roman society. Reflecting upon Plotinus' account of the body, she argues that it must be understood against the backdrop of prevailing Roman attitudes, refined in the gladiatorial games, where the audience was encouraged to identify with 'the hero's power rather than the victim's pain' (Miles 1999: 85). While Plotinus was writing some time after Seneca, the games were as much a feature of Seneca's Rome as they were of Plotinus', and were just as problematic (cf. Letter VII; Seneca 1969: 41–4). What Seneca does not suggest is that we could live without this body: he is simply reflecting upon the misery – as well as the joy – that comes from embodied existence.

Potentially more problematic are those passages where Seneca claims to be offering a way of life that is 'godlike' (Letter LIV; 1969: 103). This godlike existence is defined by freedom from care, and is seen as fulfilling the desire for the tranquil life. Nussbaum has offered her own reasons for rejecting this goal. She argues that such a lifestyle could not be understood to relate to the experience of being human, and therefore is ultimately an inappropriate model for human spirituality. Ethical virtues of the kind that we value could arise only in a life like this, where frailty, vulnerability and mortality give such concepts as bravery, strength, courage and wisdom their value (Nussbaum 1990: 374). If we are to live a truly meaningful life we should not avoid the vulnerability of existence, but accept it, throwing ourselves into this life (Nussbaum 1994b: 160).

At the same time, Nussbaum is not averse to using Seneca's ideas on the godlike life to reformulate her account of transcendence. While resisting a form of transcendence that is characterized by 'standing apart' from the physical universe, she argues for an account of the transcendent human life which locates this feature in the desire to *un-*

derstand. In this sense, there is no tension between the Stoic desire to live in accordance with nature and the desire to achieve a godlike life: 'Our nature *is* a godlike nature: for what is most godlike is to seek comprehensive understanding' (Nussbaum 1994a: 499). Similarly, Hadot suggests that philosophy is best understood as the attempt to gain the transcendent state of wisdom (Hadot [1987] 1995: 59). Yet neither Nussbaum nor Hadot propose that this form of transcendence is to be understood in contradistinction to ordinary physical human existence: it arises from it, and is part of it.

All this moves us some way further in the quest for a contemporary account of the meaningful life. Pierre Hadot has argued that a philosophy which combines Stoicism and Epicureanism provides an ideal basis for a contemporary spirituality, for these philosophies combine 'tension and relaxation, duty and serenity, moral conscience and the joy of existence' ([1987] 1995: 108). Hadot suggests that the spiritual exercises of the ancients were intended to turn us away from 'the false values of wealth, honors and pleasures' towards the values of 'virtue, contemplation, a simple life-style, and the simple happiness of existing' ([1987] 1995: 104). This seems an appropriate starting point for an account of how we might develop a contemporary vision of the meaningful life which does not descend into privatism, but which responds appropriately to the issues facing the world today. Indeed, I shall argue, it is by reflecting upon our place in the cosmos that we can become more grounded, finding in human existence a sense of depth that challenges the superficial values of a consumerist society. Hadot writes of the 'simple happiness of existing': how many of us really achieve such a lifestyle? Yet it would seem that the only satisfying way to live is through accepting our mundane existence, seeing ourselves as part of the physical universe. This is Seneca's solution to the question of how to live, and it is the application of such an idea that will inform the remainder of this book.

Conclusion

Sex, Death and the
Meaningful Life

We are now at a stage where we are able to make some tentative conclusions about the way in which reflection upon sex and death might be used to suggest a series of strategies for living the meaningful life. Throughout this study, my concern has been to start any such reflections with the recognition that we are creatures who are born, who are sexuate beings, and who are also mortal. In drawing together some of the threads that unite the disparate figures considered in this book, that fundamental acceptance of our humanity remains central.

At the outset, the relationship between transcendence and immanence must be addressed. There has been a tendency among the thinkers considered in this book to focus on one of these attributes at the expense of the other when formulating their accounts of the nature of human being. So, for Plato, to live the meaningful life involves transcending the physical. Sex and death, in this context, are spiritualized, transformed into a love that is distanced from its physical expression, and a death that acts as the gateway to life. In similar vein, Augustine argues that, to live the meaningful life, one must transcend the facts of physical existence. 'Physical existence', in this instance, is linked principally with the sexual life and reflects some of Augustine's own problems with this area of human experience. Against this backdrop, 'spirituality' becomes defined as that which distances us from the ordinary human experiences of sex and death. The meaningful life is thus grounded, not in an appreciation of and engagement with the physical, but in the attempt to transcend our physical placing. At the same time, both Plato and Augustine are concerned to highlight the problematic nature of death for any account of the meaningful life. In addressing this issue, they seek to define human being as potentially transcendent, able to resist the attraction of the immanent human life – although, as has been suggested, the pull of physical life maintains its hold, shaping Augustine's concept of God and Plato's suggestions that human relationship – and particularly human love – might be employed as a means of attaining the Good.

Such a vision of human being need not be limited to avowedly religious perspectives. Despite claims to be holding together the transcendent and immanent aspects of humanity, the existentialist ideas of Sartre and Beauvoir focus on the potentiality of a transcendent way of being which entails a resistance to the immanent nature of the physical world that ensnares consciousness. Ultimately, their attempt to incorporate both transcendence and immanence into the integrated human life fails, and, as with Augustine and Plato, it is the potential transcendence offered by consciousness which is seen to provide the basis for the meaningful life – even if the reality of death means that this life is rendered absurd.

Invariably, accounts that focus on the transcendent, however that is defined, tend to problematize the physical world, rendering it somehow alien. Yet it is not simply the quest for transcendent solutions that proves problematic when addressing the question of how one is to live a meaningful life. Engagement with Sade's philosophy showed that pursuing the 'temptation of immanence' (Clayton 2000: 390) does not necessarily lead to Utopia: far from it. Locating meaning purely in sexual pleasure leads to a superficial, and surprisingly barren, account of the possibilities open to human being. In fact, Sade cannot maintain his attempt to reject any transcendent meaning, be that located in God or Reason. The emphasis placed upon 'ordering' sexual experience and committing 'unnatural' acts suggests that, even in as self-consciously immanent a philosophy as Sade's, a kind of transcendence is being sought which comes to define the nature of human being.

A possible solution to this *impasse* is presented in the writings of Freud and Seneca. I have argued that the more literary aspects of Freud's work suggest ways of deriving value from physical life *itself*. Freud comes up with the possibility of a kind of meaning based in the fundamental mutability of human life and relationship. In his powerful sentence: 'A flower that blossoms only for a single night does not seem to us on that account less lovely'. In this sense, value is ascribed to human life not from without, but from a deep engagement with the things of the physical world. A form of transcendence develops which is dependent upon the experience of living in this physical world.

A similar trend can be identified in Seneca's thought. The rejection of dualistic ways of thinking leads to a more rounded account of human being: the physical experience of being human *and* the phenomenon of thought are linked. It is through living in this world, through an engagement with our physical placing, that we can discover a form of transcendence. In apprehending the beauty of the world around us, in human relationship, in reflection upon where we find ourselves, we can discover and engage in the meaningful life.

This leads to a further point. Must the recognition of a reflective capacity open to humanity necessarily distance us from the world, our home? For Plato, the essential self is located with the soul/mind, and thus my body is not essential to who I really am. For Augustine, the mind is where the image of God is located, and, although he resists dualistic interpretations of the relationship between mind and body, it is difficult to avoid the conclusion that the mind takes priority in his account of the self. Similarly, in Sartre, the transcendental quality of the mind leads to a vision of human being distinct from the physical world – a world which is, at times, viewed with horror.

Again, engagement with Seneca's thought suggests the possibility of an alternative perspective. Reflection is recognized as important, but in no sense is it understood as the means whereby I might affect an escape from the physical world: after all, for the Stoic, *everything* is physical. Rather, it is through engaging this reflective capacity that I share in the reflective aspects of God/Nature. Acknowledging the significance of consciousness does not mean that I must reject the reality of being a physical creature. Both aspects are significant for understanding the nature of my humanity, and for structuring a meaningful life.

Perhaps this suggests something of the struggle involved in being human; a struggle that Freud expresses in his conflictual account of the self. We are beings who exist halfway between the animals and the angels. And just as I am suggesting that we need to achieve a balance between the transcendent options and immanent experiences open to us, so we need to balance the reflective and physical parts of our selves. In this, we need to go beyond Seneca's rather ambiguous reflections on the significance of relationship. While Seneca does emphasize the importance of friendship, he suggests that we should not base too much upon such mutable relationships that are inevitably open to loss. In developing my account of the meaningful life, my emphasis will be different: to be truly happy, we need to be both reflective and relational. In other words, a balance needs to be maintained between the transcendent and immanent aspects of being human.

In seeking to ground an account of the transcendent in the physical life, death must be confronted, for it is the phenomenon of death that apparently makes human life meaningless. The obvious advantage of Plato's and Augustine's philosophies is that they lessen the challenge posed by death by placing meaning firmly outside this mutable human realm. For Plato, the Good is located in the world of ideas that transcends this world of impressions; for Augustine, happiness is possible only if one accepts and loves the eternal God who transcends the physical universe. I have wanted to avoid such a conclusion, and my sympathies are with Sartre, Beauvoir, Freud, Sade and Seneca when they refuse, in their different ways, to locate meaning outside this physical world.

Regardless of the outcome, the engagement with death is important, for it inevitably leads to a discussion of where meaning might be found. Contemporary Western culture effectively ignores death in a variety of ways, and in so doing succeeds in promoting the trivial over the profound. It is not simply the case that death provides our culture with its last taboo; death *is* spoken of, but an analysis of certain features of Western life suggest that such discussions are predicated upon the belief that it need not occur. Death is viewed as an accident that, if one adopts a suitably careful lifestyle, one might avoid. In this sense, our society seems to have adopted the position ascribed by Tolstoy to Pyotr Ivanovich in his *Death of Ivan Ilyich*. Confronted with the sudden awareness that he, like Ivan, could die at any time, he resists the fear which arises from such a thought with 'the customary reflection' that 'death were a chance experience that could happen only to Ivan Ilyich, never to himself' (Tolstoy [1886] 1981: 44). The prevalence of an insurance culture encourages such a view. This might seem an odd point to make: after all, insurance seems to be predicated upon a recognition that I could/will die, and therefore I need to ensure that my financial commitments can be fulfilled after my death. But the way in which insurance is sold suggests a different emphasis: by taking out a particular policy, it is implied that I can protect myself from the transience of life. Death is objectified and placed in a category that makes it more manageable. In the process, it becomes distanced from me. Ultimately, an illusion of control over death itself is constructed. My existence seems permanent, even necessary.

The values promoted by Western consumerism reflect a similar, somewhat paradoxical, recognition and denial of death. Surrounding oneself with desirable objects gives the impression that I am grounded in the world. The illusion of permanence derived from material objects is projected onto the self. The things I possess come not only to define who I am, but also to mask the fact that I am a mutable creature who will one day die. Chuck Palahniuk's novel *Fight Club* is shocking not simply because of the way in which it exposes the violence that lies at the heart of dominant constructions of masculinity. Palahniuk also poses a challenge to the consumerist construction of personal identity: 'the things you used to own, now they own you' (Palahniuk 1997: 44). And this is not enough to create a satisfying life. Indeed, the recognition of mortality exemplifies the ethos of the 'Fight Club' founded by Tyler Durden. Without an awareness of the possibility that one may, at any moment, die, life, it is argued, loses its meaning. The way in which violence is linked with death by Palahniuk's protagonists might rightly be resisted; but what his book suggests is something of the significance of death that has been lost by our culture. Accepting mortality provides a boundary for our experiences; it makes our decisions meaningful.

All of this necessitates that we turn again to the reality of death and the lessons that it might teach us. It is for this reason that I would resist the claims of some feminists that the paradigm of natality can simply replace that of mortality for defining human being. Human life does involve the joy of birth, of love, of human relationship. But it also involves the sorrow of death, of loss, of rejection.[1] In this sense, I would argue that human life is always potentially tragic. We find the loved one only to risk losing them to death/the other. There is a vulnerability associated with human life that must be addressed. And this sense of the tragic is vividly attested to in the writings of the figures considered in this book. Augustine graphically expresses this powerful sense of loss, before fleeing to the solution offered by a transcendent God. Human life is defined by misery; the only hope lies with God. Sartre and Beauvoir, while rejecting Augustine's solution, accept the idea that death renders life absurd. Similarly, Freud suggests that the combination of animal and 'god' in human being – the physical and the mental – contribute to a general neurosis. We are sick animals. Because of our ability to reflect, we are unable to accept our animal status and thus are unable, ultimately, to be happy. The challenge for any schema that refuses simply to adopt a straightforwardly transcendental perspective is to grapple with this realization that we are mutable beings, subject to death, open to loss.

Accepting this state of affairs is difficult, and it is important not to seek a way out of this struggle by erecting a false sense of where security or safety might be found. We live in what has been described as a 'risk society' (Beck 1992), where the language of risk assessment, appropriately applied to the workplace, has increasingly been applied to all other areas of life with startling consequences. Hélène Joffe argues that we are consistently presented with potential risks by a mass media dependent upon compelling stories for its existence.[2] For an entertainment culture (cf. Postman 1985), such stories must involve danger, real or imagined, to captivate the viewer. Risks are invariably presented in ways which suggest that 'they are systematically caused, statistically describable and, consequently, somewhat predictable' (Joffe 1999: 3). The attempt to control the transient underpins such ideas. Moreover, Joffe's study shows how the language used to describe such risks consistently links danger with 'the other' (1999: 73–89). She suggests that this reveals an important psychological mechanism for coping with perceived threats: rather than associate the threat with myself and the group with which I identify, I project that danger onto a group which I consider to be other than myself or mine.

I would wish to extend Joffe's conclusions. The attitudes that she identifies might rightly be applied to the way in which Western people approach the issue of loss, and specifically the loss associated with death. Mortality is projected away from the self and onto others. When death does occur to those identified with one's group there is a sense of outrage, and, in some cases, the attempt to attribute blame begins. Now, in some instances this will be appropriate: my contention is that the insurance culture (which increasingly characterizes Western life), in collaboration with the practice of law, extends the concept of blame inappropriately.[3] It is almost as if the word 'accident' has ceased to have any real meaning, and this suggests a degree of control over life which we simply do not possess. Death has been removed from its rightful place *in the midst of life* and is viewed increasingly as an aberration that could be avoided.

Is it possible to cope differently with the issue of loss? Rather than refusing to accept its reality, we might be better advised to employ alternative strategies. Indeed, it may be through the attempt to create meaning (by art or human activity) that we can more adequately engage with these deep and disturbing emotions. Consider the following examples: knowing that Schubert's String Quintet in C Major was composed during his final illness in 1828 can make the poignancy and drama of the opening chords of the first movement seem even more beautiful. The words of 'Solveig's song', written by Henrik Ibsen and put to music by Grieg in his *Peer Gynt,* express vividly the complex emotions of a woman awaiting her lover, not knowing whether he is alive or dead:

> The winter may pass, and spring,
> And summer too, and the whole long year.
> But some time I know that you will come,
> And I shall wait, as I promised I would . . .
> God give you joy, if you stand before His footstool.
> I shall wait here till you come back to me.
> And if it's there you're waiting,
> we shall meet there, my friend.
> (Ibsen [1867] 1987: 123–4).

Some of the most powerful passages from Shakespeare are those that reflect upon the death of loved ones and the inevitability of one's own demise. In this passage, Macbeth has just learnt of his wife's death, and his sense of loss leads to this expression of the futility of human life:

> Tomorrow, and tomorrow, and tomorrow,
> Creeps in this petty pace from day to day,
> To the last syllable of recorded time;
> And all our yesterdays have lighted fools
> The way to dusty death. Out, out, brief candle,
> Life's but a walking shadow, a poor player
> That struts and frets his hour upon the stage,
> And then is heard no more; it is a tale
> Told by an idiot, full of sound and fury,
> Signifying nothing.
> (*Macbeth*, 5.5)

Such pieces of work connect us with others who, like us, are struggling to find a way through the inevitable losses of human life. Writing or composing such pieces, or engaging with them, creates empathic connections with others in similar situations. We recognize our selves and our own challenges in these works, and our relationships are strengthened through the recognition of a common humanity, that, like us, stands in the shadows of death and loss. And this recognition need not lead to alienation and depression. Rather, it can connect us more deeply with one another. Joy and sorrow meet in such pieces, just as they meet in the day-to-day experiences of being human. Accepting, rather than resisting, the vulnerability that comes with our humanity may lead to a deeper, more profound engagement with life, and with each other, than that which resists such ideas.

All very well: but to accept such a tragic view of human life may make us feel at sea, lost in a sense of the futility and hopelessness of human life. In such a situation, we need strategies for living. Dietrich Bonhoeffer, reflecting upon the form Christianity might take in a secular world, suggested that it would consist primarily of 'prayer and righteous action' (Bonhoeffer 1979: 300), and I want to suggest a similar structure for a meaningful life that takes seriously the mutability of being human. I have argued that Seneca's Stoicism offers an account of human being which locates it in the physical universe (viz., accepts that we are animals), but which also accepts the possibility of contemplation (for we are animals who can think/reflect). Reason and nature are not distinct. Under such a reading, humanity is understood to be that part of the universe that can reflect upon itself, which is conscious of itself. This is the gift, the 'unheard of miracle' (Hadot [1987] 1995: 259) of being human. The beauty of the cosmos is something we can see and, moreover, appreciate. This brings with it a responsibility that other animals do not have. We must recognize the impact that our actions can have upon this world; we are the guardians of this world, not its owners (cf. White 1967).

Holding together the two poles of human being – contemplation and action – leads to my suggestions for constructing the meaningful life. Firstly, philosophy can be viewed as a form of therapy. Building upon the insights of the Hellenistic schools, philosophy becomes a reflective engagement with the experience of being human. This holistic practice goes some way to resisting the violent swings between transcendent and immanent interpretations of the nature of human being. Both features of our humanity are to be held together, and it is through employing the form of the spiritual exercise that we might be able to live meaningfully. These exercises were designed, Pierre Hadot argues, as cognitive therapies to change the way in which we think about our selves and our place in the world. When read in this way, the *Medita-tions* of Marcus Aurelius, for example, or the *Letters* of Seneca can be seen as presenting challenges to habitual ways of thinking. Of particu-lar significance are the exercises designed to develop a mindset that accepts the inevitability of death. Death is not viewed as something tragic or abhorrent: rather it is part of the cycle of life (Seneca 1969: 181–2). In similar vein, the Epicurean Lucretius presents the following argument: life must include death, for without death nothing new would ever be born or come about (for discussion of this argument see Nussbaum 1994a). Such ideas suggest a viewpoint that coheres with a contemporary ecological perspective. Under such accounts, death is a necessary part of the universal recycling of carbon, a process that is itself necessary for life to exist in the first place.

Reflecting upon death in this way is not a feature derivable only from the Hellenistic philosophies: parts of the Judeo-Christian tradi-tion offer similar texts which suggest that an acceptance of change and chance can lead to tranquillity. The following passage from Ecclesiastes offers a poetic account of just such an approach, which also involves placing death within its wider cosmic setting:

For everything there is a season, and a time to every purpose under heaven:
A time to be born, and a time to die; a time to plant, and a time to pluck up that which is planted;
A time to kill, and a time to heal; a time to break down, and a time to build up;
A time to weep, and a time to laugh; a time to mourn, and a time to dance;
A time to cast away stones, and a time to gather stones together; a time to embrace, and a time to refrain from embracing;
A time to get, and a time to lose; a time to keep, and a time to cast away;
A time to rend, and a time to sew; a time to keep silence, and a time to speak;
A time to love, and a time to hate; a time of war, and a time of peace.
(Ecclesiastes 3: 1–8)

Taking on board this sense that our life is defined by transience does not mean – or even necessitate – that we will not fear our own death or the deaths of those we love. Heartlessness or lack of feeling need not accompany the learning of this lesson. Rather, the intention is that by decentring the self we come to see things from a wider perspective. Rather than shoring up the self in the face of change and death, it becomes possible to throw ourselves unreservedly into life, finding in its very flux and change its meaning.

And this connects to my second suggestion. If I am advocating a contemplative approach, based upon a revisioning of philosophy as therapeutic practice, it is important that such activity is grounded in human intimacy and relationship. We are social animals, and in constructing the meaningful life we must not avoid this central issue. Of course, this opens us up to the possibility of loss, and it is interesting to note that both Augustine and Seneca, in different ways, see immuring oneself to loss as a key way of responding to the transience of human life. Yet what is valuable in human life is located in that which is vulnerable: our relationships with others. And it would be wrong to see such relationships as defined only by the possibility of loss. Much joy comes from relating to others and entering into loving relationships. And it is this relational quality that is fundamental to our humanity. Indeed, the phenomenon of sexuality suggests that the human individual can never be understood in isolation from others. Relationship and connection are fundamental to the reality of being human. Sex also draws our attention to the fact that we are dependent not only upon others for our existence, but also upon the world itself. Love, which has an eternal quality in that it can survive even death, is grounded in the reality of human touching: kissing, caressing, even intercourse. Here, in human flesh, the eternal and the mutable, mind and matter, meet, and merge.

Thomas Hardy's poem 'Transformations' suggests a bringing together of such a cosmic perspective with a fundamental acceptance of the significance of human life and relationship. Here, the recycling of matter is expressed in a way that finds room for the reality of human love:

> Portion of this yew
> Is a man my grandsire knew,
> Bosomed here at its foot:
> This branch may be his wife,
> A ruddy human life
> Now turned to a green shoot.
>
> These grasses must be made
> Of her who often prayed,
> Last century, for repose;
> And the fair girl long ago
> Whom I often tried to know

> May be entering this rose.
> So, they are not underground,
> But as nerves and veins abound
> In the growths of upper air,
> And they feel the sun and rain,
> And the energy again
> That made them what they were!
> (Hardy 1998: 68)

Hardy hints at an acceptance of the tragic reality of human life: we are destined for death and the grave. Yet accepting this fact need not mean that we are committed to an account of human existence that sees it as meaningless. The other feature that this poem highlights is the value of human relationships: love, in all its mutable messiness, is eternal. It is in this sense that the transcendent can be returned to its rightful place within the world. We can reflect upon our situation, we can derive value from the experiences we have in this world. Those things that make us most human – sex and death – can be viewed not as dangerous or to be avoided, but as sources for meaning and truth.

Notes

Introduction

1 Feminists such as Grace Jantzen (1998) would place more emphasis on birth. I have not focused specifically on this feature as I feel it can be included within a discussion of sexuality: after all, it is through sexual intercourse that new life is created. My primary concern is to pursue the habitual connection made within the Western tradition between sex and death, the one being understood as linked, irrevocably, to the other.

2 According to Plato's *Symposium*, Eros is one of the most ancient gods, possibly even the oldest (cf. Plato 1951: 42; 178b).

3 As we shall see in chapter 3, Freud echoes this idea when he links the conflicting sex- and death-drives: *eros* and *thanatos.*

4 So, figures as diverse as Plato, Sartre, Sade, and Freud suggest, albeit in different ways, that sex and death are linked with the female/feminine.

5 See H. Kramer and J. Sprenger, *Malleus Maleficarum* ([1486] 1971, 46): 'a woman is beautiful to look upon, contaminating to the touch, and deadly to keep.'

6 So, for example, both Sartre and Sade make use of this perceived connection in their philosophies.

7 We will consider Augustine's account of the significance of the Fall for understanding human being in much depth when we consider his ideas in chapter 1.

8 Readers who are interested in such a survey are directed to Jonathan Dollimore's *Death, Desire and Loss in Western Culture* (1998).

Chapter 1 Transcending Mortality

1   Val Plumwood's critique provides a good example of this trend.
2   The exclusive language used here is deliberate: as we shall see, there may
    be good grounds for assuming the Platonic philosopher will – ideally –
    be male, although it should be noted that Plato himself had female stu-
    dents.
3   For discussion of this issue, see M. E. Waithe, 'Diotima of Mantinea', in
    Waithe 1987: 83-116; and A.-M. Bowery, 'Diotima tells Socrates a story',
    in Ward 1996: 175–94.
4   For discussion of possible reasons for associating a woman with this
    account of love, see Cavarero 1995: 92–4; particularly p. 94: 'In Diotima's
    speech maternal power is annihilated by offering its language and vo-
    cabulary to the power that will triumph over it, and will build its foun-
    dations on annihilation itself.'
5   For support of this reading, see Cavarero 1995: 91.
6   Later in the *Laws* sexual intercourse between men will be forbidden (for
    discussion of this move, cf. Plato 1951: 13).
7   In the later philosophy of Aristotle such ideas will be carried into his
    account of the processes of reproduction. In *On the Generation of Ani-
    mals*, Book I, men are understood to provide the active form (reason/
    spirit) and women the passive matter that is to be shaped.
8   I am grateful to Gwen Griffith-Dickson for suggesting this reading.
9   See discussion in chapter 4.
10 For a fuller account of what this might involve, see chapter 5.
11 So, 'When Socrates had settled himself and had his dinner like the rest,
    we poured libations and sang a hymn to the god and performed all the
    customary ritual actions, and then betook ourselves to drinking' (Plato
    1951: 38; 176a).
12 For a fuller discussion of this point, see Beverley Clack, 'Embodiment
    and feminist philosophy of religion', in *Women's Philosophy Review*
    (forthcoming).
13 In this sense, Augustine builds upon some ideas of Stoic philosophy which
    will be considered in chapter 5.
14 Freud's account of the self revolves around a similar idea, only in his
    case the conflict lies between the sex- and death-drives (cf. chapter 3).
15 For a purely negative account of Augustine's anthropology, see Scott
    Mann, *Heart of a Heartless World: religion as ideology* (Montreal and
    London: Black Rose Books, 1999), pp. 294-7.
16 Reflecting on such passages and the fears of being annihilated by nature
    and the natural may go some way to explaining his horror of the wor-
    ship of Liber and Priapus (*City of God*, VI, 9).
17 For hints of a possible homosexual relationship, cf. Augustine 1961: 55.

18 Plotinus suggests that the account given of Plato above is accurate: it is possible to progress from the world to the eternal while accepting a Platonic view of the universe.

19 Cf., for example, Tertullian, *On Female Dress*, Book II, ch. 1.

20 Cf. Michel Foucault (1990) *The Care of the Self*.

21 Cf. Giulia Sissa (1991) *Greek Virginity*.

22 Cf. *De bono coniugali*, 25: 'For continence is a virtue not of the body but of the mind' (Augustine 2001a: 47).

23 For example, menstruation is seen as that flow which defies shape, and thus there are ritual laws that allow it to be shaped and thus ordered (cf. *De bono coniugali*, 23).

24 Cf. E. Pagels, 'Freedom from necessity', in G. Robbins (1988) *Genesis 1-3 in the History of Exegesis*, p. 94.

25 Cf. Jostein Gaarder's *Vita brevis* for a fictional response to Augustine's *Confessions* from his concubine that focuses largely on this aspect of his writing.

26 Cf. his satirical comment on Roman society in *City of God*, II, 20, which could so easily be applied to the mores of contemporary Western popular culture.

Chapter 2 Transcending the Void

1 These issues will be addressed in more depth in the conclusion to this book.

2 The 'for-itself' in Sartrean terminology is a being with the capacity for transcendence, the existentialist individual. The 'in-itself' in Sartrean terminology is immanent being – the world, physical existence.

3 Roger Scruton ([1986] 1994) criticizes the extent to which this idea dominates Sartre's understanding of love: 'The desire to "possess" may be a feature of love: it may even be a feature of desire. But it is not an essential feature of either' (p. 124).

4 In French, 'visqueux' is more accurately rendered as 'sticky'.

5 It is interesting to note the extent to which Sartre distances sexuality from the (heterosexual) male. Two of the examples used of 'bad faith' are sexual: the woman who avoids the issue of sex on a 'first date' by focusing only on the present moment, and the homosexual who refuses to accept that he is a 'pederast' (Sartre [1943] 1969: 55–6; 63–7). The idea that a homosexual can be equated with a pederast ('a man who commits sodomy with a boy') says much about Sartre's own prejudices. Both examples suggest that sexuality is being projected away from the subject (in this case Sartre) and on to the other.

6 For passages and criticisms, see B. Clack 1999.

7 A point that forms the focus for the discussion of Sade in chapter 4.

Chapter 3 Eros, Thanatos and the Human Self

1 Cf., for example, Ward 1998 and Loughlin 1998. For a critique of this position, see Clack 2000.

2 Features which determine the account of human being offered by thinkers as diverse as Descartes ([1637] 1968) and Sartre.

3 The emphasis on the 'unconscious' is, of course, open to the following criticism: how can we know, consciously, that the unconscious exists? This criticism forms the basis for Sartre's critique of Freud's ideas (cf. Sartre [1971] 1999: 48–55). Freud's response would undoubtedly horrify Sartre: in order to discover the unconscious we need the help of an analyst!

4 Freud's definition of eros is complex and shifting. At times he uses it to refer to the sex instinct, at others it is used more generally and with wider application as the life instinct.

5 The superego is usually understood as the internalized voice of social conscience/parental authority.

6 The use of the male pronoun is deliberate: Freud's account of human development uses the male child's experience as normative.

7 Lacan develops this aspect of Freud's thought when he considers the social function of 'the Father' (Lacan [1958] 1982).

8 In this sense, Freud stands in relation to other thinkers such as Hegel, Weininger ([1903] 1910) and Spengler ([1932] 1961), who develop the idea of a 'species consciousness', a concept which they invariably related to the female.

9 The way in which Freud weaves together science and the imagination is further exemplified in his *Moses and Monotheism* (1939), a highly creative – and controversial – work, which defies codification as science, history or fiction.

10 Norman O. Brown ([1959] 1985) focuses on this aspect of Freud's work: a human is defined as a neurotic animal, formed by repression.

11 To a degree, this has been illustrated in Sartre and Beauvoir's account of consciousness. Despite their attempts to ground this concept in physical experience, they ultimately define consciousness as that which transcends the physical.

12 More recently, Stewart Guthrie (1993) has offered a similar theory of religion that focuses on the attribution of human characteristics to non-human objects and events a strategy which makes our environment seem more friendly to us than in fact it is.

13 As Timothy Leary puts it: 'In the past, the reflexive genetic duty of top management (priests, politicians, physicians) has been to make individuals feel passive, hopeless, and unimportant in the face of death. Obedience and submission in life and death were rewarded on a consumer-fraud

time-payment plan. As a reward for sacrificing their lives in the here-and-now, individuals were promised immortality in a postmortem, gated community variously known as Heaven, Paradise, or the Kingdom of the Lord. This was, of course, a sweet deal for the rich and powerful, whose serfs and slaves would willingly postpone their pleasures and never consider rebellion since there were better times ahead after they were dead' (Leary 1997: 111–12).

14 The use of the word 'man' is deliberate here. As this section will show, the concept of humanity has been derived from male reflection upon the world, and to use an inclusive generic here – 'humanity' – would mask this fact.

15 Cf. Plato, *Phaedo*; Descartes, *Discourse on Method*; R. C. Solomon, *Continental Philosophy since 1750* on the Enlightenment formulation of the self.

16 Cf. *De Anima*.

17 Cf. Mary Pellauer's reflections on the female orgasm in Nelson and Longfellow, eds. (1994), *Sexuality and the Sacred*, pp. 149–68.

18 Freud in a letter to Kata Levy wrote of the impact of this event: 'I do not know whether cheerfulness will ever call on us again' (Gay 1995: 391–2).

19 In response to Sophie's death he wrote: 'Since I am the deepest of unbelievers, I have no one to accuse and know that there is no place where one can lodge an accusation' (Gay 1995: 393).

Chapter 4 Sex and Death in a Meaningless Universe

1 The best example of this escalation in violence is found in the fourth part of *The 120 Days of Sodom* ([1785] 1990a), where the four-month debauch is brought to its murderous conclusion.

2 In this passage, Mme Dubois gives her reasons for rejecting the notion of providence.

3 Camille Paglia describes Sade's view thus: 'Sade asks: "What is man? and what difference is there between him and other plants, between him and all the other animals of the world? None, obviously"' (Paglia 1991: 236).

4 It seems strange, then, that David Coward argues that *The Misfortunes of Virtue* is superior to its reworkings as *Justine* (1791) and *The New Justine* (1797), as these latter renditions 'add verbiage and horror but obscure the point' (Sade [1787] 1992: xxix); after all, 'the point' *is* the horror!

5 As we shall see, an alternative account of what it means to live 'according to Nature' can be given: and in this case will be exemplified by Seneca's Stoic interpretation of this phrase.

6 For example, the cannibal Minski had the women of his seraglio draped in tulle in such a manner that their breasts and buttocks were exposed, but 'their cunts were not visible at all' (Sade [1797] 1968: 603).

7 This act evidently expresses something significant for Sade, for it replicates an almost identical scene in the 1791 version of *Justine*, where, on this occasion, Justine is the victim (Sade [1791] 1990b: 730–31).

8 Compare with Augustine on the nature of evil. Evil is an absence, a lack of goodness: it is literally 'no-thing' (cf. *City of God*, Book XI, chapter 22).

9 We might think in this context of Edgar Allan Poe's comment: 'The death of a beautiful woman is, unquestionably, the most poetical topic in the world' (Hough 1965: 26).

10 See also Freud ([1905:] 1977: 71): 'The sexuality of most male human beings contains an element of *aggressiveness* – a desire to subjugate.'

11 At times, even Sade seems aware of the monotony of this repetition: 'I shall limit myself to a foreshortened account of the first month I spent in that monastery . . .; the rest would be pure repetition; the monotony of that sojourn would make my recital tedious . . .' ([1791] 1990b: 593).

12 David Coward makes a similar point in his introduction to *The Misfortunes of Virtue*: 'he was the *victim* of a moral backlash which might as easily have fallen on a score of aristocratic rakes' (Sade [1787] 1992: xvii; my emphasis).

13 The focus on how one responds to the things that happen suggests connections with Augustine's theory of the will.

14 So, 'the other disappears almost entirely, becoming merely a vehicle for the lover's personal wish and, at the same time, a permanent obstacle to its fulfillment' (Nussbaum 1994a: 177).

15 Of course, we should not ignore the fact that this does not always happen: but that should not force us to give up entirely the connection between mother and child found in other examples.

16 Chantal Thomas makes a similar point: 'To listen to the victim is to be put into the position of being *overcome* by language, of no longer *knowing* the pleasure of losing one's head' (Thomas 1995: 258).

17 Victims can be turned into survivors or, at least, be considered as individuals in their own right who are not simply identified with the oppressor/murderer's acts. I remember reading an article some time ago by the sister of one of the women murdered by Fred and Rosemary West. Her aim in writing this piece was to reassert the integrity of her sister's memory as a person in her own right, not simply as a victim of a horrific crime.

18 At least as Justine's death is presented in *Juliette*.

19 In saying this, I am following James Lovelock's account of nature in *Gaia* (1995).

20   Juliette may be a woman, but to all intents and purposes she is defined according to masculinist tastes. All of his female libertines are, as Carter puts it, simply 'female impersonators' (Carter 1979: 104).

Chapter 5 Living in Accordance with Nature

1   Although Nussbaum notes that what might be considered the more academic side of philosophy (viz., logic, metaphysics etc.) is important, for these disciplines are concerned with the attainment of truth (cf. Nussbaum 1994a: 491).
2   Cf., for example, Kant, *On the Beautiful and Sublime* (1764); Schopenhauer, 'On Women' (1851); Rousseau, *Emile* (1762).
3   Musonius Rufus, writing in the first century CE, argues that women, like men, should be able to practise philosophy (for details cf. Nussbaum 1994a: 323).
4   See also Elizabeth Asmis's largely positive appraisal of Stoicism, 'The Stoics on women' (Ward 1996: 68–92).
5   Juvenal refers to him as 'the immensely wealthy Seneca' (*Satires*, X: 16; Seneca 1969: 11).
6   For example, Nussbaum (1994a) and Griffin ([1976] 1992).
7   It is telling that at one point Sandbach comments: 'it is hard for the *Englishman* of today to approach Seneca with sympathy' (Sandbach [1989] 1994: 161; my emphasis).
8   Cf. Letter XC, where he exalts the simplicity (i.e., lack of material goods) of the golden age.
9   For details, see Nussbaum (1994b).
10   See Brian R. Clack (1999), where this argument is advanced.
11   Cf. Nussbaum (1994a: 50) for discussion of this point.
12   Cf. Chapter 15, 'Transcending humanity', of Nussbaum's *Love's Knowledge: essays on philosophy and literature* (1990): 'the valuable things in life don't come apart so neatly from the fearful and terrible' (p. 368).
13   For this reason I differ from Nussbaum's more theistic interpretation of Stoicism. She might write that their 'god is the god within' (Nussbaum 1994a: 353) but I do not think this has to be understood theistically: if anything it simply underpins the importance of taking seriously the contemplative life and the lifestyle that stems from it.
14   A standard definition of this approach to God is offered by Richard Swinburne: 'By a theist I understand a man who believes that there is a God. By a "God" I understand something like a "person without a body (i.e., a spirit) who is eternal, free, able to do anything, knows everything, is perfectly good, is the proper object of human worship and obedience, the creator and sustainer of the universe"' (Swinburne 1977: 1).
15   The use of such an example seems to undercut Jantzen's contention that

Western thinking has not been interested in natality (cf. Jantzen 1998).

16 So Foucault ([1984] 1990) shows how during this period concern for the body was as important as contemplation of the mind.

17 Indeed, Nussbaum goes so far as to argue that the Stoic teacher encourages the pupil 'to be indifferent to the injustice she suffers' (Nussbaum 1994a: 10).

18 For a similar idea, see Marcus Aurelius: 'You will vanish in that which gave you birth, or rather you will be taken up into its generative reason by the process of change' (*Meditations* IV: 14; Aurelius 1998: 26); or 'every part of me will be assigned its place by change into some part of the Universe' (*Meditations* V: 13; Aurelius 1998: 38).

19 Cf. *Meditations* VII: 32: 'either extinction or a change of abode' (Aurelius 1998: 61).

20 Such a view is also found in Plotinus: 'The life of the universe does not serve the purposes of one individual but of the whole' (Ennead, 4.4.39, quoted in Miles 1999: 81).

21 Seneca is not alone in emphasizing the significance of relationship: Marcus Aurelius writes in similar vein of the connection between all things (*Meditations*, VI: 38), and marriage is consistently supported in Stoic thought, where it is understood in terms of partnership (cf. Asmis in Ward 1996).

Conclusion

1 Writing this conclusion has been a difficult experience, as I do so in the aftermath of the destruction by terrorists of the World Trade Center in New York and part of the Pentagon building in Washington (11 September 2001). Thousands of innocent people have died, and in such a context the recognition that human life involves sorrow and loss seems so obvious as to be almost banal.

2 So, concerns that the MMR vaccination might cause autism in children have comprised a major news story in recent years. It should be noted that the media has chosen to emphasize the work of the doctor who makes this connection rather than the views of the vast majority of the medical profession who refute such a link. To emphasize supposed dangers is newsworthy; to explore the position of the majority – that this vaccination is safe – is not.

3 Television advertisements for 'no win, no fee' legal advice and action are now common, suggesting that any accident might be traced to a source who is ultimately to blame.

References and Bibliography

Airaksinen, T. (1995) *The Philosophy of the Marquis de Sade*. London: Routledge.

Annas, J. (1976) 'Plato's Republic and feminism', *Philosophy*, 51, 307–21.

Annas, J. (1981) *An Introduction to Plato's Republic*. Oxford: Clarendon Press.

Aquinas, T. *Summa Theologiae* II/II.

Ariès, P. (1976) *Western Attitudes Toward Death from the Middle Ages to the Present*, trans. P. M. Ranum. London: Marion Boyars.

Ariès, P. and A. Béjin, eds. (1986) *Western Sexuality: practice and precept in past and present times*. Oxford: Blackwell.

Aristotle (1955) *Nicomachean Ethics*, trans. J. A. K. Thomson. Harmondsworth: Penguin.

Augustine (1873) *On the Trinity*, trans. A. W. Hadden. Edinburgh: T. & T. Clark.

Augustine (1874) *On Marriage and Concupiscence*, in *The Works of Aurelius Augustine, Bishop of Hippo*, vol. 12, ed. M. Dods. Edinburgh: T. & T. Clark, 93–202.

Augustine (1961) *Confessions*, trans. R. S. Pine-Coffin. Harmondsworth: Penguin.

Augustine (1998) *City of God*, trans. R. W. Dyson. Cambridge: Cambridge University Press.

Augustine (2001a) *De bono coniugali*, trans. P. G. Walsh. Oxford: Clarendon Press.

Augustine (2001b) *De sancta uirginitate*, trans. P. G. Walsh. Oxford:

Clarendon Press.

Aurelius, M. (1998) *Meditations*, trans. A. S. L. Farquharson. Oxford: Oxford University Press.

Bacon, F. (1620) *Novum Organum*, in J. M. Robertson (1905) *The Philosophical Works of Francis Bacon*, trans. R L. Ellis and J. Spedding. London: Routledge.

Barthes, R. (1977) *Sade, Fourier, Loyola*, trans. R. Miller. London: Jonathan Cape.

Bataille, G. (1995) 'The use value of D. A. F. Sade (An open letter to my current comrades)' in *Sade and the Narrative of Transgression*, eds D .B. Allison, M. S. Roberts and A. S. Weiss. Cambridge: Cambridge University Press, 16–32.

Battersby, C. (1998) *The Phenomenal Woman*. Cambridge: Polity.

Beauvoir, S. de ([1949] 1972) *The Second Sex*, trans. H. M. Parshley. Harmondsworth: Penguin.

Beauvoir, S. de ([1981] 1985) *Adieux: a farewell to Sartre*, trans. P. O'Brian. Harmondsworth: Penguin.

Beck, U. (1992) *The Risk Society: towards a new modernity*. London: Sage.

Becker, E. (1973) *The Denial of Death*. New York: Free Press.

Beckett, S. (1990) 'Waiting for Godot', in *The Complete Dramatic Works*. London: Faber & Faber, 7–88.

Biale, D. (1992) *From Intercourse to Discourse: control of sexuality in rabbinical literature*. Berkeley, CA: Center for Hermeneutical Studies.

Blond, P. ed. (1997) *Post-Secular Philosophy*. London: Routledge.

Bonhoeffer, D. (1979) *Letters and Papers from Prison*. London: SCM.

Bowie, M. (1991) *Lacan*. London: Fontana.

Brennan, T. (1992) *The Interpretation of the Flesh: Freud and femininity*. London: Routledge.

Brown, N. O. ([1959] 1985) *Life Against Death: the psychoanalytical meaning of history*. Hanover, NH: Wesleyan University Press.

Brown, P. (1969) *Augustine of Hippo*. London: Faber & Faber.

Brown, P. (1988) *The Body and Society*. New York: Columbia University Press.

Brown, P. (2000) *Augustine of Hippo*, rev. edn. London: Faber & Faber.

Burrus, V. (1994) 'Word and flesh: the bodies and sexuality of ascetic women in Christian antiquity', in *Journal of Feminist Studies in Religion*, 10 (1), 27–52.

Bynum, C. W. (1987) *Holy Feast and Holy Fast*. Berkeley: University of California Press.

Cameron, D. and E. Frazer (1987) *The Lust to Kill*. New York: New York University Press.

Caputi, J. (1988) *The Age of Sex Crime*. London: Women's Press.

Carroll, N. (1990) *The Philosophy of Horror*. London: Routledge.

Carter, A. (1979) *The Sadeian Woman*. London: Virago.

Cavarero, A. ([1990] 1995) *In Spite of Plato*, trans. S. Anderlini-D'Onofrio and Á. O'Healy. Cambridge: Polity.

Chrysostom, J. (1979) 'Instruction and refutation directed against those men cohabiting with virgins', in E. A. Clark, *Jerome, Chrysostom and Friends*. New York: Edwin Mellen Press.

Clack, B., ed. (1999) *Misogyny in the Western Philosophical Tradition: a reader*. Basingstoke: Macmillan.

Clack, B. (2000) 'Human sexuality and the concept of God/ess', in *The Good News of the Body*, ed. L. Isherwood. Sheffield: Sheffield Academic Press, 115–133.

Clack, B. and B. R. Clack (1998) *The Philosophy of Religion: a critical introduction*. Cambridge: Polity.

Clack, B .R. (1999) *An Introduction to Wittgenstein's Philosophy of Religion*. Edinburgh: Edinburgh University Press.

Clayton, P. (2000) *The Problem of God in Modern Thought*. Grand Rapids, MI: William Eerdmans.

Collins, M. L. and C. Pierce (1980) 'Holes and slime: sexism in Sartre's psychoanalysis', in C. C. Gould and M. W. Wartofsky, *Women and Philosophy: toward a theory of liberation*. New York: Pedigree, 112–27.

Cooper, D. E. (1990) *Existentialism*. Oxford: Blackwell.

Dekkers, M. ([1997] 2000) *The Way of All Flesh: a celebration of decay*, trans. S. Marx-Macdonald. London: Harvill Press.

Descartes, R. ([1637] 1968) *Discourse on Method*, trans. F. E. Sutcliffe. Harmondsworth: Penguin.

DiCenso, J. J. (1999) *The Other Freud: religion, culture and psychoanalysis*. London: Routledge.

Dilman, I. (1987) *Love and Human Separateness*. Oxford: Blackwell.

Dollimore, J. (1998) *Death, Desire and Loss in Western Culture*. Harmondsworth: Penguin.

Dworkin, A. (1981) *Pornography: men possessing women*. London: Women's Press.

Flew, A. (1989) *An Introduction to Western Philosophy: ideas and arguments from Plato to Popper*. London: Thames & Hudson.

Foucault, M. ([1984] 1990) *The Care of the Self*, trans. R. Hurley. Harmondsworth: Penguin.

Foucault, M. (1992) *The Use of Pleasure*, trans. R. Hurley. Harmondsworth: Penguin.

Freud, S. ([1905] 1977) 'Three essays on the theory of sexuality', in *On Sexuality*. Penguin Freud Library (hereafter PFL), vol. 7.

Freud, S. ([1907] 1977) 'The sexual enlightenment of children', in *On Sexuality*. PFL vol. 7.

Freud, S. ([1908] 1985) '"Civilized" sexual morality and modern nervous illness', in *Civilization, Society and Religion*. PFL vol. 12.

Freud, S. ([1911] 1984) 'Formulations on the two principles of mental functioning', in *On Metapsychology*. PFL vol. 11.

Freud, S. ([1913] 1985) 'The theme of the three caskets', in *Art and Literature*. PFL vol. 14.

Freud, S. ([1915a] 1985) 'Thoughts for the times on war and death', in *Civilization, Society and Religion*. PFL vol. 12.

Freud, S. ([1915b] 1984) 'Instincts and their vicissitudes', in *On Metapsychology*. PFL vol. 11.

Freud, S. ([1916] 1990) 'On transience', in *Art and Literature*. PFL vol. 14.

Freud, S. ([1919] 1938) *Totem and Taboo*. Harmondsworth: Penguin.

Freud, S. ([1920] 1984) 'Beyond the pleasure principle', in *On Metapsychology*. PFL vol. 11.

Freud, S. ([1923] 1984) 'The ego and the id', in *On Metapsychology*. PFL vol. 11.

Freud, S. ([1927] 1985) 'The Future of an Illusion', in *Civilization, Society and Religion*. PFL vol. 12.

Freud, S. ([1929] 1975) *Civilization and its Discontents*. London: Hogarth Press.

Freud, S. ([1939] 1985) 'Moses and monotheism', in *The Origins of Religion*. PFL vol. 13.

Fullbrook, E. and K. Fullbrook (1993) *Simone de Beauvoir and Jean-Paul Sartre: the remaking of a twentieth century legend*. Hemel Hempstead: Harvester Wheatsheaf.

Fullbrook, E. and K. Fullbrook (1998) *Simone de Beauvoir: a critical introduction*. Cambridge: Polity.

Gaarder, J. (1997) *Vita brevis*. London: Phoenix.

Gallop, J. (1982) *Feminism and Psychoanalysis*. Basingstoke: Macmillan.

Gallop, J. (1995) 'Sade, mother and other women', in *Sade and the Narrative of Transgression*, eds. D. B. Allison, M. S. Roberts and A. S. Weiss. Cambridge: Cambridge University Press, 122–41.

Gay, P. (1995) *Freud: a life for our time*. Basingstoke: Macmillan.

Gear, N. (1963) *The Divine Demon: A portrait of the Marquis de Sade*. London: Frederick Muller.

Giddens, A. (1991) *Modernity and Self-Identity*. Cambridge: Polity.

Green, K. (1995) *The Woman of Reason: feminism, humanism and political thought*. Cambridge: Polity.

Griffin, M. ([1976] 1992) *Seneca: a Philosopher in politics*. Oxford: Oxford University Press.

Griffin, S. (1989) 'Split culture', *Readings in ecology and feminist theology*, ed, M. H. MacKinnon and M. McIntyre. Kansas City: Sheed & Ward, (1995) 25–35.

Grimshaw, J. (1986) *Feminist Philosophers: women's perspectives on philosophical traditions*. Hemel Hempstead: Harvester Wheatsheaf.

Grosz, E. (1990) *Jacques Lacan: a feminist introduction*. London: Routledge.

Guthrie, S. E. (1993) *Faces in the Clouds: a new theory of religion*. Oxford:

Oxford University Press.

Hadot, P. ([1987] 1995) *Philosophy as a Way of Life*, trans. A. I. Davidson. Oxford: Blackwell.

Hardy, T. (1998) *Selected Poems*, ed. N. Page. London: J. M. Dent.

Hénaff, M. (1995) 'The encyclopedia of excess', in *Sade and the Narrative of Transgression*, eds. D. B. Allison, M. S. Roberts and A. S. Weiss. Cambridge: Cambridge University Press, 142–70.

Hesiod (1988) *Theogony and Works and Days*, trans. M. L. West. Oxford: Oxford University Press.

Holloway, R. (1992) *Anger, Sex, Doubt and Death*. London: SPCK.

Hough, R. L., ed., (1965) *The Literary Criticism of Edgar Allan Poe*. Lincoln: University of Nebraska Press.

Hume, D. ([1779] 1947) *Dialogues Concerning Natural Religion*. Indianapolis: Bobbs-Merrill.

Ibsen, H. ([1867] 1987) *Peer Gynt and the Pretenders*, trans. M. Meyer. London: Methuen.

Irigaray, L. (1985a) *Speculum of the Other Woman*, trans. G. C. Gill. Ithaca: Cornell University Press.

Irigaray, L. (1985b) *This Sex Which is Not One*, trans. C. Porter. Ithaca: Cornell University Press.

Irigaray, L. (1992) *Elemental Passions*, trans. J. Collie and J. Still. London: Athlone Press.

Irigaray, L. (1993) *Sexes and Genealogies*, trans. G. C. Gill. New York: Columbia University Press.

Isherwood, L. and E. Stuart (1998) *Introducing Body Theology*. Sheffield: Sheffield Academic Press.

Jantzen, G. M. (1998) *Becoming Divine: towards a feminist philosophy of religion*. Manchester: Manchester University Press.

Joffe, H. (1999) *Risk and 'the Other'*. Cambridge: Cambridge University Press.

Kerr, F. (1997) *Immortal Longings: versions of transcending humanity*. London: SPCK.

Klossowski, P. (1995) 'Sade, or the philosopher-villain', in *Sade and the Narrative of Transgression*, eds D. B. Allison, M. S. Roberts and A. S. Weiss. Cambridge: Cambridge University Press, 33–61.

Kramer, H. and J. Sprenger ([1486] 1971) *The Malleus Maleficarum*, trans. M. Summers. New York: Dover.

Lacan, J. ([1958] 1982) 'The meaning of the phallus', in *Feminine Sexuality*, ed. J. Mitchell and J. Rose. London: Macmillan.

Lamb, S. and D. Sington (1998) *Earth Story: the shaping of our world*. London: BBC Books.

Larrington, C., ed. (1992) *The Feminist Companion to Mythology*. London: Pandora Press.

Lasch, C. (1985) *The Minimal Self: psychic survival in troubled times*. London: Picador.

Leary, T. (1997) *Design for Dying*. London: Thorsons.

Lingis, A. (1995) 'The Society of the Friends of Crime', in *Sade and the Narrative of Transgression*, eds D. B. Allison, M. S. Roberts and A. S. Weiss. Cambridge: Cambridge University Press, 100–21.

Lloyd, G. (1984) *The Man of Reason: 'male' and 'female' in Western philosophy*. London: Methuen.

Loughlin, G. (1998) 'Refiguring masculinity in Christ', in *Religion and Sexuality*, eds M. A. Hayes, W. Porter and D. Tombs. Sheffield: Sheffield Academic Press, 405–14.

Lovelock, J. (1995) *Gaia: a new look at life on earth*. Oxford: Oxford University Press.

Macquarrie, J. (1973) *Existentialism: an introduction, guide and assessment*. Harmondsworth: Penguin.

Marcuse, H. ([1956] 1987) *Eros and Civilization: a philosophical inquiry into Freud*. London: Ark.

Miles, M. R. (1999) *Plotinus on Body and Beauty*. Oxford: Blackwell.

Miller, N. K. (1995) 'Gender and narrative possibilities', in *Sade and the Narrative of Transgression*, eds D. B. Allison, M. S. Roberts and A. S. Weiss. Cambridge: Cambridge University Press, 213–27.

Monk, R. (1991) *Ludwig Wittgenstein: the duty of genius*. London: Vintage.

Murdoch, I. ([1953] 1967) *Sartre: romantic rationalist*. Glasgow: Fontana.

Nelson, J. (1988) *The Intimate Connection*. Philadelphia: Westminster Press.

Nelson, J. and S. P. Longfellow, eds. (1994) *Sexuality and the Sacred*. London: Mowbray.

Nussbaum, M. (1990) *Love's Knowledge: essays on philosophy and literature*. NewYork: Oxford University Press.

Nussbaum, M. (1994a) *The Therapy of Desire: theory and practice in hellenistic ethics*. Princeton, NJ: Princeton University Press.

Nussbaum, M. (1994b) 'Pity and mercy: Nietzsche's Stoicism', in *Nietzsche, Genealogy, Morality: essays on Nietzsche's On the Genealogy of Morals*, ed. R. Schacht. Berkeley: University of California Press.

Pagels, E. (1988) *Adam, Eve and the Serpent*. Harmondsworth: Penguin.

Paglia, C. (1991) *Sexual Personae*. Harmondsworth: Penguin.

Palahniuk, C. (1997) *Fight Club*. London: Vintage Books.

Pawson, J. D. (1988) *Leadership is Male*. London: Highland.

Pellauer, M. (1994) 'The Moral Significance of Female Orgasm', *Sexuality and the Sacred*, eds J. Nelson and S. Longfellow. London: Mowbray, 149–68.

Pfohl, S. (1994) 'Seven mirrors of Sade', in *The Divine Sade*, ed. D. N. Sawhney. Warwick: Warwick Journal of Philosophy.

Pilardi, J. (1999) *Simone de Beauvoir: writing the self*. Westport, Ct: Praeger.

Plato (1945) *The Republic*, trans. F. M. Cornford. Oxford: Oxford University Press.

Plato (1951) *The Symposium*, trans. W. Hamilton. Harmondsworth: Penguin.

Plato (1973) *Phaedrus*, trans. W. Hamilton. Harmondsworth: Penguin.

Plato (1977) *Timaeus*, trans. D. Lee. Harmondsworth: Penguin.

Plato (1993) *Phaedo*, trans. D. Gallop. Oxford: Oxford University Press.

Plumwood, V. (1993) *Feminism and the Mastery of Nature*. London: Routledge.

Postman, N. (1985) *Amusing Ourselves to Death*. London: Methuen.

Power, K. (1995) *Veiled Desire: Augustine's writing on women*. London: DLT.

Ranke-Heinemann, U. (1991) *Eunuchs for the Kingdom of Heaven*. Harmondsworth: Penguin.

Robbins, G., ed. (1988) *Genesis 1–3 in the History of Exegesis*. New York: Edwin Mellen.

Rose, G. (1992) *The Broken Middle*. Oxford: Blackwell.

Rycroft, C. (1971) *Reich*. London: Fontana.

Ryle, G. ([1949] 1963) *The Concept of Mind*. Harmondsworth: Penguin.

Sade, D.-A.-F., Marquis de ([1787] 1992) *The Misfortunes of Virtue and Other Early Tales*, trans. D. Coward. Oxford: Oxford University Press.

Sade, D.-A.-F., Marquis de ([1785] 1990a) *The 120 Days of Sodom*, trans. A. Wainhouse and R. Seaver. London: Arrow Books.

Sade, D.-A.-F., Marquis de ([1791] 1990b) *Justine, Or Good Conduct Well Chastised*, in *Justine, Philosophy in the Bedroom, & Other Writings*. New York: Grove Press.

Sade, D.-A.-F., Marquis de ([1795] 1995) *Philosophy in the Boudoir*, trans. Meredith X. London: Creation Books.

Sade, D.-A.-F., Marquis de ([1797] 1968) *Juliette*, trans. A. Wainhouse. New York: Grove Press.

Sandbach, F. H. ([1989] 1994) *The Stoics*, rev. 2nd edn. Indianapolis: Hackett.

Sartre, J.-P. ([1938] 1965) *Nausea*, trans. R. Baldick. Harmondsworth: Penguin.

Sartre, J.-P. ([1943] 1969) *Being and Nothingness: an essay on phenomenological ontology*, trans. H. E. Barnes. London: Methuen.

Sartre, J.-P. ([1946] 1985) *Existentialism and Human Emotions*, trans. B Frechtman and H. E. Barnes. New York: Castle.

Sartre, J.-P. ([1971] 1999) *Sketch for a Theory of the Emotions*, trans. P. Mairet. London: Routledge.

Sawhney, D. N. (1994) 'A manner of thinking', in *The Divine Sade*, ed. D. N. Sawhney. Warwick: Warwick Journal of Philosophy.

Scruton, R. ([1986] 1994) *Sexual Desire: a philosophical investigation*. London: Phoenix.

Seneca, L. A. (1969) *Letters from a Stoic*, trans. R. Campbell. Harmondsworth: Penguin.

Seneca, L. A. (1995a) 'On anger', *Moral and political essays*, trans. J. M. Cooper and J. F. Procopé. Cambridge: Cambridge University Press, 1–116.

Seneca, L. A. (1995b) 'On mercy', *Moral and political essays*, trans. J. M. Cooper and J. F. Procopé. Cambridge: Cambridge University Press, 117–64.

152   *References and Bibliography*

Seneca, L. A. (1995c) 'On the private life', *Moral and Political Essays*, trans. J. M. Cooper and J. F. Procopé. Cambridge: Cambridge University Press 165–80.

Seneca, L. A. (1995d) 'On favours', *Moral and Political Essays*, trans. J. M Cooper and J. F. Procopé, Cambridge: Cambridge University Press, 181–308.

Seneca, L.A. (1997a) *Dialogues and Letters*, trans. C. D. N. Costa, Harmondsworth: Penguin.

Seneca, L. A. (1997b) 'Consolation to Helvia', *Dialogues and Letters*, trans. C. D. N. Costa, Harmondsworth: Penguin, 3–28.

Seneca, L. A. (1997c) 'On tranquillity of mind', *Dialogues and Letters*, tr. C. D. N. Costa, Harmondsworth: Penguin, pp. 29–58.

Seneca, L.A. (1997d) 'On the shortness of life', *Dialogues and Letters*, trans. C. D. N. Costa. Harmondworth: Penguin, 59–83.

Shaw, G. (1987) *God in our Hands*. London: SCM.

Shuttle, P. and P. Redgrove (1986) *The Wise Wound*. London: Paladin.

Simons, M. A. (1986) 'Beauvoir and Sartre: the philosophical relationship', *Yale French Studies*, 72, 165–79.

Sissa, G. (1991) *Greek Virginity*. Cambridge, MA: Harvard University Press.

Soskice, J. M. (1992) 'Love and attention', *Philosophy, Religion and the Spiritual Life*, ed. M. McGhee. Cambridge: Royal Institute of Philosophy, 59–72.

Solomon, R.C. (1988) *Continental Philosophy since 1750: The Rise and Fall of the Self*. Oxford: OUP.

Spengler, O. ([1932] 1961) *The Decline of the West*, trans. H. Werner. London: George Allen & Unwin.

Stewart, R. M., ed. (1995) *Philosophical Perspectives on Sex and Love*. Oxford: Oxford University Press.

Suleiman, S. R., ed. (1986) *The Female Body in Western Culture: contemporary perspectives*. Cambridge, MA: Harvard University Press.

Swinburne, R. (1977) *The Coherence of Theism*. Oxford: Clarendon Press.

Tacitus (1977) *Annals of Imperial Rome*, trans. M. Grant. Harmondsworth: Penguin.

Tarnas, R. (1991) *The Passion of the Western Mind*. London: Pimlico.

Tertullian (1869) 'On female dress',*The Writings of Tertullian*, vol. 1, trans. S. Thelwall. Edinburgh: T. & T. Clark.

Thomas, C. (1995) 'Fantasizing Juliette', in *Sade and the Narrative of Transgression*, eds D. B. Allison, M. S. Roberts and A. S. Weiss. Cambridge: Cambridge University Press, 251–64.

Tolstoy, L. ([1886] 1981) *The Death of Ivan Ilyich*, trans. L. Solotaroff. New York: Bantam.

Trible, P. (1978) *God and the Rhetoric of Sexuality*. Philadelphia: Fortress Press.

Turcan, R. ([1992] 1996) *The Cults of the Roman Empire*, trans. A. Nevill.

Oxford: Blackwell.

Unamuno, M. de (1921) *The Tragic Sense of Life*. London: Macmillan.

Waithe, M. E., ed. (1987) *A History of Women Philosophers*, vol. 1. Dordrecht: Kluwer Academic Press.

Ward, G. (1998) 'The gendered body of the Jewish Jesus', in *Religion and Sexuality*, eds M. A. Hayes, W. Porter and D. Tombs. Sheffield: Sheffield Academic Press, 170–92.

Ward, J. K., ed. (1996) *Feminism and Ancient Philosophy*. London: Routledge.

Warner, M. (1990) *Alone of All her Sex*, 2nd ed. London: Picador.

Weininger, O. ([1903] 1910) *Sex and Character*. London: Heinemann.

Welch, S. D. (1990) *A Feminist Ethic of Risk*. Minneapolis: Fortress Press.

White, L. (1967) 'The historical roots of our ecologic crisis', in *Readings in Ecology and Feminist Theology*, ed. M. H. MacKinnon and M. M. McIntyre. Kansas City: Sheed & Ward,(1995), 25–35.

Williams, R. (2000) *Lost Icons: reflections on cultural bereavement*. Edinburgh: T. & T. Clark.

Index